THE TABLE TALK OF

MARTIN LUTHER

THE TABLE TALK OF

MARTIN LUTHER

Edited with an Introduction by
THOMAS S. KEPLER

BAKER BOOK HOUSE
Grand Rapids, Michigan

Copyright 1952 by
The World Publishing Company
Reprinted 1979 by
Baker Book House Company

Library of Congress Catalog
Card Number: 52-10322

ISBN: 0-8010-5408-7

Second printing, November 1981

PHOTOLITHOPRINTED BY CUSHING - MALLOY, INC.
ANN ARBOR, MICHIGAN, UNITED STATES OF AMERICA

CONTENTS

Introduction

THE FORMAL beginning of Protestantism can be dated as occurring on the eve of All Saints Day, 1517, when Martin Luther nailed his ninety-five theses on the church door at Wittenberg. In performing this act, he was not so much attacking indulgences directly as showing their uselessness and their ineffectiveness. His own words give insight into the meaning of this event; he maintained

> That the pope could release no punishments but what he inflicted, and indulgences could be nothing but a relaxation of ecclesiastical penalties; that they affected only the living; that the dead were not subject to canonical penances, and so could receive no benefits by indulgences; and that such as were in purgatory could not by them be delivered from the punishment of their sins; that indeed the pope did not grant indulgences to the dead, by virtue of the power of the keys, but by way of suffrage; that indulgences seldom remit all punishment; that those who believe they shall be saved by indulgences only, shall be damned

with their masters; that contrition can procure remission of the fault and punishment without indulgences, but that indulgences can do nothing without contrition; that the pope's indulgence is not to be condemned, because it is the declaration of a pardon obtained of God, but only to be preached with caution, lest the people should think it preferable to good works; that Christians should be instructed, how much better it is to abound in works of mercy and charity to the poor, than to purchase a pardon; and that it is a matter of indifference either to buy, or not to buy, an indulgence; that indulgences are not to be trusted to; that it is hard to say what the treasure of the church is, which is said to be the foundation of indulgences; that it is not the merits of Christ or his saints, because they produce grace in the inner man; and crucify the outward man, without the pope's interposing; that this treasure can be nothing but the power of the keys, or the gospel of the glory and grace of God; that indulgences cannot remit the most venial sin in respect of guilt; that they remit nothing to them who by a sincere contrition have a right to perfect remission; and that Christians are to be exhorted to seek pardon of their sins

by the pains and labour of penance, rather than
to get them discharged without reason.

Luther's reflection upon forgiveness of one's sins
through repentance and labor of penance shows
the depth of his spirit. While Luther is well known
for his abilities in organization and scholarship, he
should be best known for his religious piety. The
depth of his religious experience was catching in
the lives of those who knew him. Born to a peasant
family in Eisleben, Luther was encouraged by his
father to pursue law at the University of Erfurt.
Here he studied philosophy and law, read the ancient classics, and received his master's degree at
twenty before taking up civil law. However, when
struck by lightning which killed his companion,
Luther forsook law and entered a monastery of
Augustinian hermits in July, 1505. In 1507 he cele-
brated his first mass upon being ordained a priest.
He became a lecturer at the University of Wittenberg in philosophy and biblical studies, being made
a doctor of divinity at thirty years of age.

Luther's hunger for piety was especially fed by
the writings of Augustine, Bernard of Clairvaux,
Johannes Tauler, and *Theologia Germanica* (the
anonymous writing of "The Friends of God," which

Luther published in 1518). But most of all the
Bible spoke to the spirit of Luther. Chief among
Martin Luther's lectures at Wittenberg were those
on Paul's "Letter to the Romans." It was this letter
which greatly affected his theological viewpoint
and caused him to become the great adherent of
"justification by faith." As Luther dramatically
shifted from his position of a priest in the Roman
Catholic Church to that of the chief instigator of
the Reformation, his ideas in religion showed a
number of new tendencies: Each man was to be
his own priest who could immediately approach
God; the sermon became an important part of the
church service by which God's grace aroused faith
in the hearer; hymns were sung in public worship; the sacraments were diminished to two, baptism and the Lord's Supper, since only those two
are mentioned in the New Testament; the Bible
as "the Word of God," rather than the authority
of the Pope and the Church, became the guide for
man; marriage was encouraged among the clergy;
salvation by faith in Jesus Christ was at the heart
of Christian thought and living.

Martin Luther was a tireless worker and a pro-
lific writer; his *Works* (*Werke*) vie in size with a
series of modern encyclopedias. His translation of

the New Testament into the German language, while at the Wartburg Castle, and published in September, 1522, brought the Bible to the common people; it also laid the pattern for German literature. Among the many writings of Luther, *Table Talk* is a lengthy compendium which gives his views on many subjects. The thoughts for this volume were collected by his friends and followers, chiefly by John Aurifaber (Goldschmidt) and Antony Lauterbach. From notes of Luther's discourses, his observations and opinions as his friends knew him at the table, on walks, or in the performance of his clerical duties, the basis of this book took form. Luther made a great impression on his friends: "The reporters were brim-full of zeal: whatever 'the man of God' uttered was forthwith entered upon their tablets. They were with him at his uprising and his down-lying; they looked over his shoulder as he read or wrote his letters; did he utter an exclamation of pain or of pleasure, of joy or of sorrow, down it went: did he aspirate a thought above a breath, it was caught by the intent ear of one or other of the listeners, and committed to paper."

John Aurifaber at Eisleben in 1566 brought out the first German edition of *Table Talk* (*Tisch-*

reden) ; by 1568 it had gone through its fourth reprinting. In 1569 a new edition with added materials, and edited by John Fink, appeared with this appendix: "Of prophecies which the venerable man of God, just before his holy death, delivered unto divers learned theologians and ecclesiastics, with many consolatory letters, opinions, narratives, replies, etc., never made public." This volume, dedicated to the Council of Rauschenburg on March 24, 1568, apparently contained various ideas from Luther's books and writings as discovered through the research of a Halle preacher named George Walther. Further editions, no longer extant, were published in Eiseleben in 1569 and 1577.

In 1571 another edition by Andrew Stangwald appeared, being reprinted in 1590, and dedicated to the Council of Mulhausen. Stangwald in his preface complained of defective matter and typographical errors in previous editions, which he attempted to correct. Other German editions followed from time to time, but it was not until 1743 that J. G. Walch included *Table Talk* in the collection of Luther's German *Werke*. *Table Talk*, however, never was inserted into the Latin works of Luther.

The first English translation of *Table Talk* was made by Captain Henry Bell in 1645, the House of

Commons on February 24, 1646, giving order for the printing of the volume. The copy of the order of the House of Commons reads as follows:

24TH FEBRUARY, 1646

Whereas Captain Henry Bell has strangely discovered and found a book of Martin Luther's, called his Divine Discourses, which was for a long time very marvellously preserved in Germany: the which book, the said Henry Bell, at his great costs and pains, hath translated into the English out of the German tongue, which translation and substance thereof is approved by Reverend Divines of the Assembly, as appears by a certificate under their hands:

It is ordered and ordained by the Lords and Commons assembled in parliament, that the said Henry Bell shall have the sole disposal and benefit of printing the said book, translated into English by him as aforesaid, for the space of fourteen years, to commence the date thereof. And that none do print or reprint the same, but such as shall be licensed by the said captain by authority under his hand.

(*Vera Copia*)   HENRY ELSYNG

Captain Bell's narrative about his concern for *Table Talk* reveals his enthusiasm for this volume which he translated. In part he says:

I, Captain Henry Bell, do hereby declare, both to the present age, and also to posterity, that being employed beyond the seas in state affairs divers years together, both by king James, and also by the late king Charles, in Germany, I did hear and understand, in all places, great bewailing and lamentation made by reason of the destroying and burning of above fourscore thousand of Martin Luther's books entitled, "His Last Divine Discourses."

For after such time as God stirred up the spirit of Martin Luther to detect the corruptions and abuses of popery, and to preach Christ, and clearly to set forth the simplicity of the gospel, many kings, princes, and states, imperial cities, and Hans-towns, fell from popish religion, and became protestants, as their posterities still are, and remain to this very day.

And for the further advancement of the great work of reformation then begun, the aforesaid princes, and the rest did then order, that the said Divine Discourses of Luther should forthwith be

*printed; and that every parish should have and
receive one of the foresaid printed books into
every church throughout all their principalities
and dominions, to be chained up, for the common people to read therein. . . .*

*Whereupon I took the said book before me,
and many times began to translate the same, but
I was always hindered. Then about six weeks
after I had received the said book, it fell out, that
I being in bed with my wife one night, between
twelve and one of the clock, she being asleep, but
myself awake, there appeared unto me an ancient
man, standing at my bedside, arrayed all in white,
having a long and broad white beard hanging
down at his girdle steed, who taking me by my
right ear, spake these words following unto me:
"Sirrah! will not you take time to translate that
book which is sent unto you out of Germany? I
will shortly provide for you both place and time
to do it." And then he vanished away out of my
sight. . . .*

*Then about a fortnight after I had seen that
vision, on a Sunday, I went to Whitehall to hear
a sermon; after which ended, I returned to my
lodging, which was then at King-street, at Westminster, and sitting down to dinner with my wife,*

two messengers were sent from the whole coun-
cilboard, with a warrant to carry me to the keeper
of the Gatehouse, Westminster, there to be safely
kept, until further order from the lords of the
council; which was done without showing me
any cause at all wherefore I was committed.
Upon which said warrant I was kept ten whole
years close prisoner, where I spent five years
thereof about the translating of the said book;
insomuch as I found the words very true which
the old man, in the aforesaid vision, did say unto
me—"I will shortly provide for you both place
and time to translate it."

Captain Bell had been imprisoned for pressing
the Lord Treasurer for arrears of pay. Toward the
end of his imprisonment, when the translation was
finished, the Archbishop of Canterbury, William
Laud, sent for the book to peruse. After a careful
reading of the book Archbishop Laud highly
praised the volume to the king, recommending
the book to be circulated throughout the whole
kingdom, as it was in Germany. Soon Captain Bell
was set free by the whole House of Lords, since
the king had interceded in his behalf. But fortunes
were to turn again, as Archbishop Laud fell into

troubles and was beheaded after a short imprisonment in the London Tower. A committee, however,
was appointed by the House of Commons to inspect
Captain Bell's translation. On November 10, 1645,
the committee reported the excellency of the English translation, and on February 24, 1646, the
House of Commons ordered its printing.

In the preface to this first English edition, published in 1652, a letter to the translator is prefixed.
In one paragraph of the letter are these words of
commendation: "We should, indeed, seek in vain
elsewhere for more striking and interesting speci-
mens of the talents, the disposition, and the manners of the great Reformer, than in this volume
of his 'Table Talk.' And certainly if the personal
character of any individual deserves to be dwelt
upon, it is that of Luther. In no other instance have
such great events depended upon the courage, sa-
gacity, and energy of a single man, nor can there
be found a more profitable study than the temper
and peculiarities of one, who, by his sole and un-
assisted efforts, made his solitary cell the heart and
centre of the most wonderful and important commotion the world ever witnessed; who, by the native
force and vigour of his genius, attacked and suc-
cessfully resisted, and at length overthrew the most

awful and sacred authority that ever imposed its
commands on mankind."

In recent years Ernest Kroker in six large volumes has collected 7075 speeches of Luther, and
has arranged them in the most exact possible order.
This chronological arrangement has increased the
value of *Table Talk* as historical sources. The recording of these table talks began in 1531, possibly
in 1529. Many of these conversations were originally
taken by students in shorthand in Latin and German. These students would sit around Luther and
his famous guests, recording what they could of
Luther's words. Sometimes Luther would ask them
to write down something he wished to say. Luther's
wife once jokingly told the students that they should
pay to hear his conversations in the manner they
paid to hear lectures at the university!

"It was as much the purpose of *Table Talk* to
benefit the hearers spiritually as to cheer them up
and amuse them." Some of Luther's statements
about the papacy, the antichrist, councils, excommunication, his adversaries, the Jews and Turks, do
not necessarily deal with highest spiritual values.
Some of his ideas on subjects such as astronomy
and astrology, princes and potentates, idolatry,

belong to the religious atmosphere of the sixteenth
century. Both of these types of material are de-
leted from this volume, which is mainly concerned
with Luther's conversations about high spiritual
values. Luther's table talk on the great spiritual
verities sounds a deep religious note. His statements
on such themes can be placed among high devo-
tional literature. The purpose of this volume, based
upon the translation of William Hazlitt (1778–
1830), is to let Martin Luther's insights into spiritual truths speak to the needs of modern man.
Though some of his ideas may be attached to the
sixteenth century of western Europe, many of his
spiritual suggestions in *Table Talk* sound a sane
and inspiring note for those living in the contemporary world.

Martin Luther's life was open to the high inspiration offered him from the past. Psalm 46,
called "the sublime song of faith," and written in
a time of Jewish national calamity after the Baby-
lonian exile, encouraged Luther at the time of the
Reformation. As this psalm showed the Jewish
people that their chief source of courage and
strength abode in God, so Martin Luther felt this
support in his day. Inspired by this lofty psalm, he

wrote his great hymn, "A Mighty Fortress Is Our God." Though a man of great physical vigor, he realized that his main support lay in God's grace,

> *Therefore in God I place my trust,*
> *My own claim denying.*
> *Believe in him alone I must,*
> *On his sole grace relying.*
> *He pledged to me his plighted word.*
> *My comfort is in what I heard.*
> *Therefore will I hold forever.*

The great reformer felt that music was one of the greatest means to make the worshiper aware of God's grace. In 1524 he brought out a hymnbook of twenty-three hymns to be used in public and private worship. "I always loved music," Luther remarked. "Whoso has skill in this art, is of a good temperament fitted for all things. We should not ordain young men as preachers, unless they have been well exercised in music. The singing of hymns is a goodly thing and pleasing to God. Music is a goodly thing and pleasing to God. Music is a noble gift of God, next to theology. I would not change my little knowledge of music for a great deal."

The strong faith which Luther held in God, and

the deep joy of the Christian religion as expressed in his enthusiasm for music, show themselves again and again in the religious theme in *Table Talk*. "Luther did the work of more than five men," says a contemporary biographer of the reformer. *Table Talk* shows the breadth of Luther's interests, and reveals that, in his busy life which he followed, he had time to converse with his friends on numerous topics, most of which were closely related to the central values of the Christian religion.

The text of this volume is based on the English translation of William Hazlitt (1778–1830), British literary critic and essayist. Hazlitt's translation has proved itself the most clear and accurate text of *Table Talk* in English, and the one usually resorted to in editions of Luther's conversations.

THOMAS S. KEPLER

OF GOD'S WORD

· 1 ·

THAT the Bible is God's word and book I prove thus: All things that have been, and are, in the world, and the manner of their being, are described in the first book of Moses on the creation; even as God made and shaped the world, so does it stand to this day. Infinite potentates have raged against his book, and sought to destroy and uproot it—king Alexander the Great, the princes of Egypt and of Babylon, the monarchs of Persia, of Greece, and of Rome, the emperors Julius and Augustus—but they nothing prevailed; they are all gone and vanished, while the book remains, and will remain for ever and ever, perfect and entire, as it was declared at the first. Who has thus helped it—who has thus protected it against such mighty forces? No one, surely, but God himself, who is the master of all things. And 'tis no small miracle how God has so long preserved and protected this book; for the devil and the world are sore foes to it. I believe that the devil has destroyed many good books of the church, as,

3

aforetime, he killed and crushed many holy persons, the memory of whom has now passed away; but the Bible he was fain to leave subsisting. In like manner have baptism, the sacrament of the altar, of the true body and blood of Christ, and the office of preaching remained unto us, despite the infinitude of tyrants and heretic persecutors. God, with singular strength, has upheld these things; let us, then. baptize, administer the sacrament, and preach, fearless of impediment. Homer, Virgil, and other noble, fine, and profitable writers, have left us books of great antiquity; but they are nought to the Bible.

While the Romish church stood, the Bible was never given to the people in such a shape that they could clearly, understandingly, surely, and easily read it, as they now can in the German translation, which, thank God, we have prepared here at Wittenberg.

· 2 ·

The Holy Scriptures are full of divine gifts and virtues. The books of the heathen taught nothing of faith, hope, or charity; they present no idea of these things; they contemplate only the present, and that which man, with the use of his material reason, can grasp and comprehend. Look not therein for aught of hope or trust in God. But see how the Psalms and the Book of Job treat of faith, hope, resignation, and prayer; in a word, the Holy Scripture is the highest and best of books, abounding in comfort under all afflictions and trials. It teaches us to see, to feel, to grasp, and to comprehend faith, hope, and charity, far otherwise than mere human reason can; and when evil oppresses us, it teaches how these virtues throw light upon the darkness, and how, after this poor, miserable existence of ours on earth, there is another and an eternal life.

· 3 ·

St. Jerome, after he had revised and corrected the Septuagint, translated the Bible from Hebrew into Latin; his version is still used in our church. Truly, for one man, this was work enough and to spare. *Nulla enim privata persona tantum efficere potuisset.* 'Twould have been quite as well had he called to his aid one or two learned men, for the Holy Ghost would then have more powerfully manifested itself unto him, according to the words of Christ: "Where two or three are gathered together in my name, there am I in the midst of them." Interpreters and translators should not work alone; for good *et propria verba* do not always occur to one mind.

· 4 ·

We ought not to criticise, explain, or judge the
Scriptures by our mere reason, but diligently, with
prayer, meditate thereon, and seek their meaning.
The devil and temptations also afford us occasion
to learn and understand the Scriptures, by experience and practice. Without these we should never
understand them, however diligently we read and
listened to them. The Holy Ghost must here be our
only master and tutor; and let youth have no shame
to learn of that preceptor. When I find myself assailed by temptation, I forthwith lay hold of some
text of the Bible, which Jesus extends to me; as this:
that he died for me, whence I derive infinite hope.

· 5 ·

Let us not lose the Bible, but with diligence, in
fear and invocation of God, read and preach it.
While that remains and flourishes, all prospers with
the state; 'tis head and empress of all arts and faculties. Let but divinity fall, and I would not give a
straw for the rest.

· 6 ·

The school divines with their speculations in holy
writ, deal in pure vanities, in mere imaginings de-

rived from human reason. Bonaventura, who is full
of them, made me almost deaf. I sought to learn in
his book, how God and my soul shall become reconciled, but got no information from him. They
talk much of the union of the will and understanding, but 'tis all idle fantasy. The right, practical
divinity is this: Believe in Christ, and do thy duty
in that state of life to which God has called thee.
In like manner, the *Mystical divinity of Dionysius*
is a mere fable and lie. With Plato he chatters:
Omnia sunt non ens, et omnia sunt ens—(all is
something, and all is nothing)—and so leaves
things hanging.

· 7 ·

Dr. Justus Jonas remarked at Luther's table:
There is in the Holy Scriptures a wisdom so pro-
found, that no man may thoroughly study it or
comprehend it. "Ay," said Luther, "we must ever
remain scholars here; we cannot sound the depth of
one single verse in Scripture; we get hold but of
the A B C, and that imperfectly. Who can so exalt
himself as to comprehend this one line of St. Peter:
'Rejoice, inasmuch as ye are partakers of Christ's
sufferings.' Here St. Peter would have us rejoice in

our deepest misery and trouble, like as a child kisses the rod."

· 8 ·

I have many times essayed thoroughly to investigate the Ten Commandments, but at the very outset, "I am the Lord thy God," I stuck fast; that very one word, I, put me to a *non-plus*. He that has but one word of God before him, and out of that word cannot make a sermon, can never be a preacher. I am well content that I know, however little, of what God's word is, and take good heed not to murmur at my small knowledge.

· 9 ·

I have grounded my preaching upon the literal word; he that pleases may follow me; he that will not may stay. I call upon St. Peter, St. Paul, Moses, and all the Saints, to say whether they ever fundamentally comprehended one single word of God, without studying it over and over and over again. The Psalm says: *His understanding is infinite.* The saints, indeed, know God's word, and can discourse of it, but the practice is another matter; therein we shall ever remain scholars.

The school theologians have a fine similitude hereupon, that it is as with a sphere or globe, which, lying on a table, touches it only with one point, yet it is the whole table which supports the globe. Though I am an old doctor of divinity, to this day I have not got beyond the children's learning—the Ten Commandments, the Belief, and the Lord's Prayer; and these I understand not so well as I should, though I study them daily, praying, with my son John and my daughter Magdalen. If I thoroughly appreciated these first words of the Lord's Prayer, *Our Father, which art in Heaven,* and really believed that God, who made heaven and earth, and all creatures, and has all things in his hand, was my Father, then should I certainly conclude with myself, that I also am a lord of heaven and earth, that Christ is my brother, Gabriel my servant, Raphael my coachman, and all the angels my attendants at need, given unto me by my heavenly Father, to keep me in the path, that unawares I knock my foot against a stone. But that our faith may be exercised and confirmed, our heavenly Father suffers us to be cast into dungeons, or plunged in water. So we may see how finely we understand these words, and how belief shakes, and

how great our weakness is, so that we begin to think
—Ah, who knows how far that is true which is set
forth in the Scriptures?

· 10 ·

No greater mischief can happen to a Christian
people, than to have God's word taken from them,
or falsified, so that they no longer have it pure and
clear. God grant we and our descendants be not
witnesses of such a calamity.

· 11 ·

When we have God's word pure and clear, then
we think ourselves all right; we become negligent,
and repose in a vain security; we no longer pay
due heed, thinking it will always so remain; we do
not watch and pray against the devil, who is ready
to tear the Divine word out of our hearts. It is with
us as with travellers, who, so long as they are on
the highway, are tranquil and heedless, but if they
go astray into woods or cross paths, uneasily seek
which way to take, this or that.

· 12 ·

The great men and the doctors understand not the

word of God, but it is revealed to the humble and
to children, as is testified by the Saviour in the
Gospel according to St. Matthew, xi. 25: "O Father,
Lord of heaven and earth, because thou hast hid
these things from the wise and prudent, and hast
revealed them unto babes." Gregory says, well and
rightly, that the Holy Scripture is a stream of running water, where alike the elephant may swim, and
the lamb walk without losing its feet.

· 13 ·

The great unthankfulness, contempt of God's
word, and wilfulness of the world, make me fear
that the divine light will soon cease to shine on
man, for God's word has ever had its certain course.

In the time of the kings of Judah, Baal obscured
the brightness of God's word, and it became hard
labour to destroy his empire over the hearts of men.
Even in the time of the apostles, there were heresies,
errors, and evil doctrines spread abroad by false
brethren. Next came Arius, and the word of God
was hidden behind dark clouds, but the holy fathers,
Ambrose, Hilary, Augustin, Athanasius, and others,
dispersed the obscurity. Greece and many other
countries have heard the word of God, but have

since abandoned it, and it is to be feared even now
it may quit Germany, and go into other lands. I
hope the last day will not be long delayed. The
darkness grows thicker around us, and godly servants of the Most High become rarer and more rare.
Impiety and licentiousness are rampant throughout
the world, and we live like pigs, like wild beasts,
devoid of all reason. But a voice will soon be heard
thundering forth: *Behold, the bridegroom cometh.*
God will not be able to bear this wicked world
much longer, but will come, with the dreadful day,
and chastise the scorners of his word.

· 14 ·

Kings, princes, lords, any one will needs understand the gospel far better than I, Martin Luther,
ay, or even than St. Paul; for they deem themselves
wise and full of policy. But herein they scorn and
contemn, not us, poor preachers and ministers, but
the Lord and Governor of all preachers and ministers, who has sent us to preach and teach, and who
will scorn and contemn them in such sort, that they
shall smart again; even He that says: "Whoso heareth you, heareth me; and whoso toucheth you.
toucheth the apple of mine eye." The great ones
would govern, but they know not how.

· 15 ·

Dr. Justus Jonas told Dr. Martin Luther of a noble and powerful Misnian, who above all things occupied himself in amassing gold and silver, and was so buried in darkness, that he gave no heed to the five books of Moses, and had even said to Duke John Frederic, who was discoursing with him upon the gospel: "Sir, the gospel pays no interest." "Have you no grains?" interposed Luther; and then told this fable:—"A lion making a great feast, invited all the beasts, and with them some swine. When all manner of dainties were set before the guests, the swine asked: 'Have you no grains?'" "Even so," continued the doctor, "even so, in these days, it is with our epicureans: we preachers set before them, in our churches, the most dainty and costly dishes, as everlasting salvation, the remission of sins, and God's grace; but they, like swine, turn up their snouts, and ask for guilders: offer a cow nutmeg, and she will reject it for old hay. This reminds me of the answer of certain parishioners to their minister, Ambrose R. He had been earnestly exhorting them to come and listen to the Word of God: 'Well,' said they, 'if you will tap a good barrel of beer for us, we'll come with all our hearts and hear you.' The gospel at Wittenberg is like unto the

rain which, falling upon a river, produces little
effect; but descending upon a dry, thirsty soil, ren-
ders it fertile."

· 16 ·

Some one asked Luther for his psalter, which was
old and ragged, promising to give him a new one
in exchange; but the doctor refused, because he was
used to his own old copy, adding: "A local memory
is very useful, and I have weakened mine in translating the Bible."

· 17 ·

Our case will go on, so long as its living advocates, Melancthon, and other pious and learned persons, who apply themselves zealously to the work,
shall be alive; but, after their death, 'twill be a sad
falling off. We have an example before us, in Judges
ii. 10: "And also all that generation were gathered
unto their fathers; and there arose another generation after them, which knew not the Lord, nor yet
the works which he had done for Israel." So, after
the death of the apostles, there were fearful fallings
off; nay, even while they yet lived, as St. Paul complains, there was falling off among the Galatians,
the Corinthians, and in Asia. We shall be occasioned

much suffering and loss by the Sacramentarians, the Anabaptists, the Antinomians, and other sectaries.

· 18 ·

Oh! how great and glorious a thing it is to have before one the Word of God! With that we may at all times feel joyous and secure; we need never be in want of consolation, for we see before us, in all its brightness, the pure and right way. He who loses sight of the Word of God, falls into despair; the voice of heaven no longer sustains him; he follows only the disorderly tendency of his heart, and of world vanity, which lead him on to his destruction.

· 19 ·

Christ, in Matthew, v., vi., vii., teaches briefly these points: first, as to the eight happinesses or blessings, how every Christian ought particularly to live as it concerns himself; secondly, of the office of teaching, what and how a man ought to teach in the church, how to season with salt and enlighten, reprove, and comfort, and exercise the faith; thirdly, he confutes and opposes the false expounding of the law; fourthly, he condemns the wicked hypo-critical kind of living; fifthly, he teaches what are upright and good works; sixthly, he warns men of false doctrine; seventhly, he clears and solves what might be found doubtful and confused; eighthly, he condemns the hypocrites and false saints, who abuse the precious word of grace.

· 20 ·

St. Luke describes Christ's passion better than the rest; John is more complete as to Christ's works; he describes the audience, and how the cause was handled, and how they proceeded before the seat of judgment, and how Christ was questioned, and for what cause he was slain.

When Pilate asked him: "Art thou the king of the Jews?" "Yea," said Christ, "I am; but not such a king as the emperor is, for then my servants and armies would fight and strive to deliver and defend me; but I am a king sent to preach the gospel, and give record of the truth, which I must speak." "What!" said Pilate, "art thou such a king, and hast thou a kingdom that consists in word and truth? then surely thou canst be no prejudice to me." Doubtless Pilate took our Saviour Christ to be a simple, honest, ignorant man, one perchance come out of a wilderness, a simple fellow, a hermit, who knew or understood nothing of the world, or of government.

· 21 ·

In the writings of St. Paul and St. John is a surpassing certainty, knowledge, and *plerophoria*. They write as if all they narrate had been already done before their eyes.

Christ rightly says of St. Paul, he shall be a chosen instrument and vessel unto me; therefore he was made a doctor, and therefore he spake so certainly of the cause. Whoso reads Paul may, with a safe conscience, build upon his words; for my part, I never read more serious writings.

St. John, in his gospel, describes Christ, that he is a true and natural man, *à priori*, from former time: "In the beginning was the word;" and "Whoso honoureth me, the same honoureth also the Father." But Paul describes Christ, *à posteriori et effectu*, from that which follows, and according to the actions or works, as, "They tempted Christ in the wilderness;" Take heed, therefore, to yourselves," &c.

· 22 ·

In the book of the Judges, the valiant champions and deliverers are described, who were sent by God, believing and trusting wholly in him, according to the first commandment; they committed themselves, their actions, and enterprises to God, and gave him thanks: they relied only upon the God of heaven, and said: Lord God, thou hast done these things, and not we; to thee only be the glory. The book of the Kings is excellent—a hundred times better than the Chronicles, which constantly pass over the most important facts, without any details whatever.

The book of Job is admirable; it is not written only touching himself, but also for the comfort and consolation of all sorrowful, troubled, and perplexed hearts, who resist the devil. When he conceived that God began to be angry with him, he became impatient, and was much offended; it vexed and grieved him that the ungodly prospered so well. Therefore it should be a comfort to poor Christians that are persecuted and forced to suffer, that in the life to come, God will give unto them exceeding great and glorious benefits, and everlasting wealth and honour.

· 23 ·

We need not wonder that Moses so briefly described the history of the ancient patriarchs, when we see that the Evangelists, in the shortest measure, describe the sermons in the New Testament, running briefly through them, and giving but a touch of the preachings of John the Baptist, which, doubtless, were the most beautiful.

. 24 .

Saint John the Evangelist speaks majestically, yet with very plain and simple words; as where he says: "In the beginning was the Word, and the Word was with God, and the Word was God. The same was in the beginning with God. All things were made by him, and without him was not anything made that was made. In him was life, and the life was the light of man. And the light shineth in darkness, and the darkness comprehendeth it not."

See how he describes God the Creator, and also his creatures, in plain, clear language, as with a sunbeam. If one of our philosophers or high learned men had described them, what wonderful swelling and high-trotting words would he have paraded, *de ente et essentiâ*, so that no man could have understood what he meant. 'Tis a great lesson, how mighty divine truth is, which presses through, though she be hemmed in ever so closely; the more she is read, the more she moves and takes possession of the heart.

· 25 ·

The psalms of David are of various kinds—didactic, prophetic, eucharistic, catechetic. Among the prophetic, we should particularly distinguish the 110th, *Dixit Dominus;* and among the didactic, the *Miserere Mei, De profundis,* and *Domine, exaudi orationem.* The 110th is very fine. It describes the kingdom and priesthood of Jesus Christ, and declares him to be the King of all things, and the intercessor for all men; to whom all things have been remitted by his Father, and who has compassion on us all. 'Tis a noble psalm; if I were well, I would endeavour to make a commentary on it.

· 26 ·

Dr. Luther was asked whether the history of the rich man and Lazarus was a parable or an actual fact? He replied: The earlier part of the story is evidently historical; the persons, the circumstances, the existence of the five brothers, all this is given in detail. The reference to Abraham is allegorical, and highly worthy of observation. We learn from it that there are abodes unknown to us, where the souls of men are; secrets into which we must not inquire. No mention is made of Lazarus' grave; whence we may judge, that in God's eyes, the soul

occupies far more place than the body. Abraham's
bosom is the promise and assurance of salvation,
and the expectation of Jesus Christ; not heaven
itself, but the expectation of heaven.

· 27 ·

Before the Gospel came among us, men used to
undergo endless labour and cost, and make dangerous journeys to St. James of Compostella, and
where not, in order to seek the favour of God. But
now that God, in his Word, brings his favour unto
us gratis, confirming it with his sacraments, saying,
Unless ye believe, ye shall surely perish, we will
have none of it.

· 28 ·

I have lived to see the greatest plague on earth—
the contemning of God's word, a fearful thing,
surpassing all other plagues in the world; for thereupon most surely follow all manner of punishments,
eternal and corporal. Did I desire for a man all
bitter plagues and curses, I would wish him the
contemning of God's word, for he would then have
them all at once come upon him, both inward and
outward misfortunes. The contemning of God's
word is the forerunner of God's punishments; as

the examples witness in the times of Lot, of Noah, and of our Saviour.

· 29 ·

Whoso acknowledges that the writings of the Evangelists are God's word, with him we are willing to dispute; but whoso denies this, with him we will not exchange a word; we may not converse with those who reject the first principles.

· 30 ·

In all sciences, the ablest professors are they who have thoroughly mastered the texts. A man, to be a good jurisconsult, should have every text of the law at his fingers' ends; but in our time, the attention is applied rather to glosses and commentaries. When I was young, I read the Bible over and over and over again, and was so perfectly acquainted with it, that I could, in an instant, have pointed to any verse that might have been mentioned. I then read the commentators, but I soon threw them aside, for I found therein many things my conscience could not approve, as being contrary to the sacred text. 'Tis always better to see with one's own eyes than with those of other people.

· 31 ·

The words of the Hebrew tongue have a peculiar
energy. It is impossible to convey so much so briefly
in any other language. To render them intelligibly,
we must not attempt to give word for word, but only
aim at the sense and idea. In translating Moses, I
made it my effort to avoid Hebraisms; 'twas an
arduous business. The wise ones, who affect greater
knowledge than myself on the subject, take me to
task for a word here and there. Did they attempt
the labour I have accomplished, I would find a hundred blunders in them for my one.

· 32 ·

A fiery shield is God's Word; of more substance
and purer than gold, which, tried in the fire, loses
nought of its substance, but resists and overcomes
all the fury of the fiery heat; even so, he that believes God's Word overcomes all, and remains secure everlastingly, against all misfortunes; for this
shield fears nothing, neither hell nor the devil.

· 33 ·

I never thought the world had been so wicked,
when the Gospel began, as now I see it is; I rather

hoped that every one would have leaped for joy
to have found himself freed from the filth of the
pope, from his lamentable molestations of poor
troubled consciences, and that through Christ they
would by faith obtain the celestial treasure they
sought after before with such vast cost and labour,
though in vain. And especially I thought the bishops
and universities would with joy of heart have received the true doctrines, but I have been lamentably deceived. Moses and Jeremiah, too, complained
they had been deceived.

· 34 ·

The thanks the world now gives to the doctrine
of the gospel, is the same it gave to Christ, namely,
the cross; 'tis what we must expect. This year is the
year of man's ingratitude: the next will be the year
of God's chastisement; for God must needs chastise,
though 'tis against his nature: we will have it so.

· 35 ·

Ah, how impious and ungrateful is the world,
thus to contemn and persecute God's ineffable grace!
And we—we ourselves—who boast of the gospel, and
know it to be God's Word, and recognise it for
such, yet hold it in no more esteem and respect than

we do Virgil or Terence. Truly, I am less afraid of
the pope and his tyrants, than I am of our own
ingratitude towards the Word of God: 'tis this will
place the pope in his saddle again. But, first, I hope
the day of judgment will come.

· 36 ·

God has his measuring lines and his canons,
called the Ten Commandments; they are written
in our flesh and blood: the sum of them is: "What
thou wouldst have done to thyself, the same do thou
to another." God presses upon this point, saying:
"Such measure as thou metest, the same shall be
measured to thee again." With this measuring line
has God marked the whole world. They that live
and do thereafter, well it is with them, for God
richly rewards them in this life.

· 37 ·

Is it true that God speaks himself with us in the
Holy Scriptures? thou that doubtest this, must
needs think in thy heart that God is a liar, one that
says a thing, and performs it not; but thou mayest
be sure when he opens his mouth, it is as much
as three worlds. God, with one sole word, moulded
the whole world. In Psalm xxxiii. it is said: "When

he speaketh, it is done; when he commandeth, it standeth fast."

· 38 ·

We must make a great difference between God's Word and the word of man. A man's word is a little sound, that flies into the air, and soon vanishes; but the Word of God is greater than heaven and earth, yea, greater than death and hell, for it forms part of the power of God, and endures everlastingly; we should, therefore, diligently study God's Word, and know and assuredly believe that God himself speaks unto us. This was what David saw and believed, who said: "God spake in his holiness, thereof I am glad." We should also be glad; but this gladness is oftentimes mixed up with sorrow and pain, of which, again, David is an example, who underwent manifold trials and tribulations in connection with the murder and adultery he had committed. It was no honeymoon for him, when he was hunted from one place to another, to the end he might after remain in God's .fear. In the second Psalm he says: "Serve the Lord with fear, and rejoice with trembling."

· 39 ·

The student of theology has now far greater advantages than students ever before had; first, he has the Bible, which I have translated from Hebrew into German, so clearly and distinctly, that any one may readily comprehend it; next, he has Melancthon's *Common-place Book* (Loci Communes), which he should read over and over again, until he has it by heart. Once master of these two volumes, he may be regarded as a theologian whom neither devil nor heretic can overcome; for he has all divinity at his fingers' ends, and may read, understandingly, whatsoever else he pleases. Afterwards, he may study Melancthon's Commentary on Romans, and mine on Deuteronomy and on the Galatians, and practise eloquence.

We possess no work wherein the whole body of theology, wherein religion, is more completely summed up, than in Melancthon's *Common-place Book*; all the Fathers, all the compilers of sentences, put together, are not to be compared with this book. 'Tis, after the Scriptures, the most perfect of works. Melancthon is a better logician than myself; he argues better. My superiority lies rather in the rhetorical way. If the printers would take my advice, they would print those of my books which set forth doctrine,—as my commentaries on Deuteronomy, on Galatians, and the sermons on the

four books of St. John. My other writings scarce
serve better purpose than to mark the progress of
the revelation of the gospel.

· 40 ·

Christ (Luke viii.) says, "Unto you it is given to
know the mysteries of the kingdom of God." Here
a man might ask, What mystery is that? If a mystery, why do ye preach it? Whereunto I answer:
A mystery is a thing hidden and secret; the mysteries of the kingdom of God are such things as
lie hidden in the kingdom of God; but he that
knows Christ aright, knows what God's kingdom
is, and what therein is to be found. They are mysteries, because secret and hidden from human sense
and reason, when the Holy Ghost does not reveal
them; for though many hear of them, they neither
conceive nor understand them. There are now many
among us who preach of Christ, and hear much
spoken of him, as that he gave himself to death for
us, but this lies only upon the tongue, and not in
the heart; for they neither believe it, nor are sensible of it; as St. Paul says: "The natural man
perceiveth not the things of the Spirit of God."

Those on whom the Spirit of God falls, not only
hear and see it, but also receive it within their hearts

and believe, and therefore it is no mystery or secret to them.

· 41 ·

Twas a special gift of God that speech was given to mankind; for through the Word, and not by force, wisdom governs. Through the Word people are taught and comforted, and thereby all sorrow is made light, especially in cases of the conscience. Therefore God gave to his church an eternal Word to hear, and the sacraments to use. But this holy function of preaching the Word is, by Satan, fiercely resisted; he would willingly have it utterly suppressed, for thereby his kingdom is destroyed.

Truly speech has wonderful strength and power, that through a mere word, proceeding out of the mouth of a poor human creature, the devil, that so proud and powerful spirit, should be driven away, shamed and confounded.

The sectaries are so impudent, that they dare to reject the word of the mouth; and to smooth their damnable opinions, say: No external thing makes one to be saved; the word of the mouth and the sacraments are external things: therefore they make us not to be saved. But I answer: We must discriminate wholly between the external things of

God and the outward things of man. The external
things of God are powerful and saving; it is not so
with the outward things of man.

· 42 ·

God alone, through his word, instructs the heart,
so that it may come to the serious knowledge how
wicked it is, and corrupt and hostile to God. Afterwards God brings man to the knowledge of God,
and how he may be freed from sin, and how, after
this miserable, evanescent world, he may obtain life
everlasting. Human reason, with all its wisdom, can
bring it no further than to instruct people how to
live honestly and decently in the world, how to keep
house, build, &c., things learned from philosophy
and heathenish books. But how they should learn to
know God and his dear Son, Christ Jesus, and to
be saved, this the Holy Ghost alone teaches through
God's word; for philosophy understands nought of
divine matters. I don't say that men may not teach
and learn philosophy; I approve thereof, so that
it be within reason and moderation. Let philosophy
remain within her bounds, as God has appointed,
and let us make use of her as of a character in a
comedy; but to mix her up with divinity may not
be endured; nor is it tolerable to make faith an

accidens or quality, happening by chance; for such words are merely philosophical,—used in schools and in temporal affairs, which human sense and reason may comprehend. But faith is a thing in the heart, having its being and substance by itself, given of God as his proper work, not a corporal thing, that may be seen, felt, or touched.

· 43 ·

We must know how to teach God's word aright, discerningly, for there are divers sorts of hearers; some are struck with fear in the conscience, are perplexed, and awed by their sins, and, in apprehension of God's anger, are penitent; these must be comforted with the consolations of the gospel. Others are hardened, obstinate, stiff-necked, rebel-hearted; these must be affrighted by the law, by examples of God's wrath: as the fires of Elijah, the deluge, the destruction of Sodom and Gomorrah, the downfall of Jerusalem. These hard heads need sound knocks.

· 44 ·

The gospel of the remission of sins through faith in Christ, is received of few people; most men little regard the sweet and comfortable tidings of the gos-

pel; some hear it, but only even so as they hear
mass in popedom; the majority attend God's word
out of custom, and, when they have done that, think
all is well. The case is, the sick, needing a physician,
welcome him; but he that is well, cares not for him,
as we see by the Canaanitish woman in Matthew
xv., who felt her own and her daughter's necessities,
and therefore ran after Christ, and in nowise would
suffer herself to be denied or sent away from him.
In like manner, Moses was fain to go before, and
learn to feel sins, that so grace might taste the
sweeter. Therefore, it is but labour lost (how familiar and loving soever Christ be figured unto us),
except we first be humbled through the acknowledgment of our sins, and so yearn after Christ, as
the *Magnificat* says: "He filled the hungry with
good things, and the rich he hath sent empty away,"
words spoken for the comfort of all, and for instruction of miserable, poor, needful sinners, and contemned people, to the end that in all their deepest
sorrows and necessities they may know with whom
to take refuge and seek aid and consolation.

But we must take fast hold on God's Word, and
believe all true which that says of God, though
God and all his creatures should seem unto us other
than as the Word speaks, as we see the Canaanitish

woman did. The Word is sure, and fails not, though heaven and earth must pass away. Yet, oh! how hard is this to natural sense and reason, that it must strip itself naked, and abandon all it comprehends and feels, depending only upon the bare Word. The Lord of his mercy help us with faith in our necessities, and at our last end, when we strive with death.

· 45 ·

Heaven and earth, all the emperors, kings, and princes of the world, could not raise a fit dwelling-place for God; yet, in a weak human soul, that keeps his Word, he willingly resides. Isaiah calls heaven the Lord's seat, and earth his footstool; he does not call them his dwelling-place; when we seek after God, we shall find him with them that keep his Word. Christ says: "If a man love me, he will keep my words, and my Father will love him, and we will come unto him, and make our abode with him." Nothing could be simpler or clearer than these words of the Saviour, and yet he confounds herewith all the wisdom of the worldly-wise. He sought to speak *non in sublimi sed humili genere.* If I had to teach a child, I would teach him in the same way.

· 46 ·

Great is the strength of the divine Word. In the epistle to the Hebrews, it is called "a two-edged sword." But we have neglected and contemned the pure and clear Word, and have drunk not of the fresh and cool spring; we are gone from the clear fountain to the foul puddle, and drunk its filthy water; that is, we have sedulously read old writers and teachers, who went about with speculative reasonings, like the monks and friars.

The words of our Saviour Christ are exceeding powerful; they have hands and feet; they outdo the utmost subtleties of the worldly-wise, as we see in the gospel, where Christ confounds the wisdom of the Pharisees with plain and simple words, so that they knew not which way to turn and wind themselves. It was a sharp syllogism of his: "Give unto Caesar the things which are Caesar's;" wherewith he neither commanded nor prohibited, but snared them in their own casuistry.

· 47 ·

Where God's Word is taught pure and unfalsified, there is also poverty, as Christ says: "I am sent to preach the Gospel to the poor." More than enough has been given to unprofitable, lazy, ungodly people in monasteries and cells, who lead us into danger of body and soul; but not one farthing is given, willingly, to a Christian teacher. Superstition, idolatry, and hypocrisy, have ample wages, but truth goes a begging.

· 48 ·

When God preaches his word, then presently follows the cross to godly Christians; as St. Paul testifies: "All that will live a godly life in Christ Jesus, must suffer persecution." And our Saviour: "The disciple is not greater than the master: have they persecuted me? they will persecute you also." The work rightly expounds and declares the Word, as the prophet Isaiah: Grief and sorrow teach how to mark the Word. No man understands the Scriptures, unless he be acquainted with the cross.

· 49 ·

In the time of Christ and the apostles, God's Word was a word of doctrine, which was preached everywhere in the world; afterwards in the popedom it was a word of reading, which they only read, but understood not. In this our time, it is made a word of strife, which fights and strives; it will endure its enemies no longer, but remove them out of the way.

· 50 ·

Like as in the world a child is an heir only because
it is born to inherit, even so, faith only makes such
to be God's children as are born of the Word, which
is the womb wherein we are conceived, born, and
nourished, as the prophet Isaiah says. Now, as
through such a birth we become God's children
(wrought by God without our help or doing), even
so, we are also heirs, and being heirs, are freed from
sin, death, and the devil, and shall inherit everlasting life.

· 51 ·

I admonish every pious Christian that he take not
offence at the plain, unvarnished manner of speech
of the Bible. Let him reflect that what may seem
trivial and vulgar to him, emanates from the high
majesty, power, and wisdom of God. The Bible is
the book that makes fools of the wise of this world;
it is understood only of the plain and simple hearted.
Esteem this book as the precious fountain that can
never be exhausted. In it thou findest the swaddling-
clothes and the manger whither the angels directed
the poor, simple shepherds; they seem poor and
mean, but dear and precious is the treasure that lies
therein.

· 52 ·

The ungodly papists prefer the authority of the church far above God's Word; a blasphemy abominable and not to be endured; wherewith, void of all shame and piety, they spit in God's face. Truly, God's patience is exceeding great, in that they be not destroyed; but so it always has been.

· 53 ·

In times past, as in part of our own, 'twas dangerous work to study, when divinity and all good arts were contemned, and fine, expert, and prompt wits were plagued with sophistry. Aristotle, the heathen, was held in such repute and honour, that whoso undervalued or contradicted him, was held, at Cologne, for an heretic; whereas they themselves understood not Aristotle.

· 54 ·

In the apostles' time, and in our own, the gospel was and is preached more powerfully and spread further than it was in the time of Christ; for Christ had not such repute, nor so many hearers as the apostles had, and as now we have. Christ himself says to his disciples: Ye shall do greater works than I; I am but a little grain of mustard-seed; but ye shall be like the vine-tree, and as the arms and boughs wherein the birds shall build their nests.

· 55 ·

All men now presume to criticise the gospel. Almost every old doting fool or prating sophist must, forsooth, be a doctor in divinity. All other arts and sciences have masters, of whom people must learn, and rules and regulations which must be observed and obeyed; the Holy Scripture only, God's word, must be subject to each man's pride and presumption; hence, so many sects, seducers, and offences.

· 56 ·

I did not learn my divinity at once, but was constrained by my temptations to search deeper and deeper; for no man, without trials and temptations, can attain a true understanding of the Holy Scriptures. St. Paul had a devil that beat him with fists, and with temptations drove him diligently to study the Holy Scripture. I had hanging on my neck the pope, the universities, all the deep-learned, and the devil; these hunted me into the Bible, wherein I sedulously read, and thereby, God be praised, at length attained a true understanding of it. Without such a devil, we are but only speculators of divinity,

and according to our vain reasoning, dream that so
and so it must be, as the monks and friars in monasteries do. The Holy Scripture of itself is certain and
true: God grant me grace to catch hold of its just
use.

OF GOD'S WORKS

· 57 ·

ALL the works of God are unsearchable and unspeakable, no human sense can find them out; faith
only takes hold of them without human power or
aid. No mortal creature can comprehend God in his
majesty, and therefore did he come before us in the
simplest manner, and was made man, ay, sin, death,
and weakness.

In all things, in the least creatures, and in their
members, God's almighty power and wonderful
works clearly shine. For what man, how powerful,
wise, and holy soever, can make out of one fig a fig-
tree, or another fig? or, out of one cherry-stone, a
cherry, or a cherry-tree? or what man can know

how God creates and preserves all things, and makes them grow.

Neither can we conceive how the eye sees, or how intelligible words are spoken plainly, when only the tongue moves and stirs in the mouth; all which are natural things, daily seen and acted. How then should we be able to comprehend or understand the secret counsels of God's majesty, or search them out with our human sense, reason, or understanding. Should we then admire our own wisdom? I, for my part, admit myself a fool, and yield myself captive.

· 58 ·

In the beginning, God made Adam out of a piece of clay, and Eve out of Adam's rib: he blessed them, and said: "Be fruitful and increase"—words that will stand and remain powerful to the world's end. Though many people die daily, yet others are ever being born, as David says in his psalm: "Thou sufferest men to die and go away like a shadow, and sayest, Come again ye children of men." These and other things which he daily creates, the ungodly blind world see not, nor acknowledge for God's wonders, but think all is done by chance and haphazard, whereas, the godly, wheresoever they cast their eyes, beholding heaven and earth, the air and water, see and acknowledge all for God's wonders; and, full of astonishment and delight, laud the Creator, knowing that God is well pleased therewith.

· 59 ·

For the blind children of the world the articles of faith are too high. That three persons are one only God; that the true Son of God was made man; that in Christ are two natures, divine and human, &c., all this offends them, as fiction and fable. For just as unlikely as it is to say, a man and a stone are one person, so it is unlikely to human sense and reason that God was made man, or that divine and human natures, united in Christ, are one person. St. Paul showed his understanding of this matter, though he took not hold of all, in Colossians: "In Christ dwelleth all the fulness of the Godhead bodily." Also: "In him lies hid all treasure of wisdom and knowledge."

· 60 ·

When one asked, where God was before heaven was created? St. Augustin answered: He was in himself. When another asked me the same question, I

said: He was building hell for such idle, presumptuous, fluttering and inquisitive spirits as you. After
he had created all things, he was everywhere, and
yet he was nowhere, for I cannot take hold of him
without the Word. But he will be found there where
he has engaged to be. The Jews found him at Jerusalem by the throne of grace, (Exod. xxv.) We find
him in the Word and faith, in baptism and the sacraments; but in his majesty, he is nowhere to be
found.

It was a special grace when God bound himself
to a certain place where he would be found, namely,
in that place where the tabernacle was, towards
which they prayed; as first, in Shilo and Sichem,
afterwards at Gibeon, and lastly at Jerusalem, in
the temple.

The Greeks and heathens in after times imitated
this, and built temples for their idols in certain
places, as at Ephesus for Diana, at Delphos for
Apollo, &c. For, where God built a church there the
devil would also build a chapel. They imitated the
Jews also in this, namely, that as the Most Holiest
was dark, and had no light, even so and after the
same manner, did they make their shrines dark
where the devil made answer. Thus is the devil ever
God's ape.

· 61 ·

God is upright, faithful, and true, as he has shown, not only in his promises, through Christ, of forgiveness of sins, and deliverance from everlasting death, but also, in that he has laid before us, in the Scriptures, many gracious and comforting examples of great and holy saints, who of God were highly enlightened and favoured, and who, notwithstanding, fell into great and heavy sins.

Adam, by his disobedience, hereditarily conveyed sin and death upon all his posterity. Aaron brought a great sin upon Israel, insomuch that God would have destroyed her. David also fell very heavily. Job and Jeremiah cursed the day wherein they were born. Jonas was sorely vexed, because Nineveh was not destroyed. Peter denied, Paul persecuted Christ.

These and such like innumerable examples does Holy Writ relate to us; not that we should live securely, and sin, relying upon the mercy of God, but that, when we feel his anger, "which will surely follow upon the sins," we should not despair, but remember these comfortable examples, and thence conclude, that, as God was merciful unto them, so likewise he will be gracious unto us, out of his mere goodness and mercy shown in Christ, and will not impute our sins unto us.

We may also see by such examples of great holy
men falling so grievously, what a wicked, crafty,
and envious spirit the devil is, a very prince and god
of the world.

These high, divine people, who committed such
heavy sins, fell, through God's counsel and permis-
sion, to the end they should not be proud or boast
themselves of their gifts and qualities, but should
rather fear. For, when David had slain Uriah, had
taken from him his wife, and thereby given cause
to God's enemies to blaspheme, he could not boast
he had governed well, or shown goodness; but he
said: "I have sinned against the Lord," and with
tears prayed for mercy. Job also acknowledgingly
says: "I have spoken foolishly, and therefore do I
accuse myself, and repent."

· 62 ·

When God contemplates some great work, he begins it by the hand of some poor, weak, human creature, to whom he afterwards gives aid, so that the
enemies who seek to obstruct it, are overcome. As
when he delivered the children of Israel out of the
long, wearisome, and heavy captivity in Egypt, and
led them into the land of promise, he called Moses,

to whom he afterwards gave his brother Aaron as an assistant. And though Pharaoh at first set himself hard against them, and plagued the people worse than before, yet he was forced in the end to let Israel go. And when he hunted after them with all his host, the Lord drowned Pharaoh with all his power in the Red Sea, and so delivered his people.

Again, in the time of Eli the priest, when matters stood very evil in Israel, the Philistines pressing hard upon them, and taking away the Ark of God into their land, and when Eli, in great sorrow of heart, fell backwards from his chair and broke his neck, and it seemed as if Israel were utterly undone. God raised up Samuel the prophet, and through him restored Israel, and the Philistines were overthrown.

Afterwards, when Saul was sore pressed by the Philistines, so that for anguish of heart he despaired and thrust himself through, three of his sons and many people dying with him, every man thought that now there was an end of Israel. But shortly after, when David was chosen king over all Israel, then came the golden time. For David, the chosen of God, not only saved Israel out of the enemies' hands, but also forced to obedience all kings and people that set themselves against him, and helped the kingdom up again in such manner, that in his and Solomon's time it was in full flourish, power, and glory.

Even so, when Judah was carried captive to Babylon, then God selected the prophets Ezekiel, Haggai, and Zachariah, who comforted men in their distress and captivity; making not only promise of their return into the land of Judah, but also that Christ should come in his due time.

Hence we may see that God never forsakes his people, nor even the wicked; though, by reason of their sins, he suffer them a long time to be severely punished and plagued. As also, in this our time, he has graciously delivered us from the long, wearisome, heavy, and horrible captivity of the wicked pope. God of his mercy grant we may thankfully acknowledge this.

· 63 ·

God could be rich readily enough, if he were more provident, and denied us the use of his creatures; let him, for ever so short a while, keep back the sun, so that it shine not, or lock up air, water, or fire, ah! how willingly would we give all our wealth to have the use of these creatures again.

But seeing God so liberally heaps his gifts upon

us, we claim them as of right; let him deny them if he dare. The unspeakable multitude of his benefits obscures the faith of believers, and much more so, that of the ungodly.

· 64 ·

When God wills to punish a people or a kingdom, he takes away from it the good and godly teachers and preachers, and bereaves it of wise, godly, and honest rulers and counsellors, and of brave, upright, and experienced soldiers, and of other good men. Then are the common people secure and merry; they go on in all wilfulness, they care no longer for the truth and for the divine doctrine; nay, they despise it, and fall into blindness; they have no fear or honesty; they give way to all manner of shameful sins, whence arises a wild, dissolute, and devilish kind of living, as that we now, alas! see and are too well cognizant of, and which cannot long endure. I fear the axe is laid to the root of the tree, soon to cut it down. God of his infinite mercy take us graciously away, that we may not be present at such calamities.

· 65 ·

God gives us sun and moon and stars, fire and

water, air and earth, all creatures, body and soul, all manner of maintenance, fruits, grain, corn, wine, whatever is good for the preservation and comfort of this temporal life; moreover he gives unto us his all-saving Word, yea, himself.

Yet what gets he thereby? Truly, nothing, but that he is wickedly blasphemed, and that his only Son is contemned and crucified, his servants plagued, banished, persecuted, and slain. Such a godly child is the world; woe be to it.

· 66 ·

God very wonderfully entrusts his highest office to preachers that are themselves poor sinners who, while teaching it, very weakly follow it. Thus goes it ever with God's power in our weakness; for when he is weakest in us, then is he strongest.

· 67 ·

How should God deal with us? Good days we cannot bear, evil we cannot endure. Gives he riches unto us? then are we proud, so that no man can live by us in peace; nay, we will be carried upon heads and shoulders, and will be adored as gods. Gives he poverty unto us? then are we dismayed, impatient, and murmur against him. Therefore, nothing were better for us, than forthwith to be covered over with the shovel.

· 68 ·

Since God, said some one, knew that man would not continue in the state of innocence, why did he create him at all? Dr. Luther laughed, and replied: The Lord, all-powerful and magnificent, saw that he should need in his house, sewers and cess-pools; be assured he knows quite well what he is about. Let us keep clear of these abstract questions, and consider the will of God such as it has been revealed unto us.

· 69 ·

Dr. Henning asked: "Is reason to hold no authority at all with Christians, since it is to be set aside in matters of faith?" The Doctor replied: Before faith and the knowledge of God, reason is mere darkness; but in the hands of those who believe, 'tis an excellent instrument. All faculties and gifts are pernicious, exercised by the impious; but most salutary when possessed by godly persons.

· 70 ·

God deals strangely with his saints, contrary to

all human wisdom and understanding, to the end, that those who fear God and are good Christians, may learn to depend on invisible things, and through mortification may be made alive again; for God's Word is a light that shines in a dark place, as all examples of faith show. Esau was accursed, yet it went well with him; he was lord in the land, and priest in the church; but Jacob had to fly, and dwell in poverty in another country.

God deals with godly Christians much as with the ungodly, yea, and sometimes far worse. He deals with them even as a house-father with a son and a servant; he whips and beats the son much more and oftener than the servant, yet, nevertheless, he gathers for the son a treasure to inherit, while a stubborn and a disobedient servant he beats not with the rod, but thrusts out of doors, and gives him nothing of the inheritance.

· 71 ·

God is a good and gracious Lord; he will be held for God only and alone, according to the first commandment: "Thou shalt have none other Gods but me." He desires nothing of us, no taxes, subsidies, money, or goods; he only requires that he may be our God and Father, and therefore he be-

stows upon us, richly, with an overflowing cup, all
manner of spiritual and temporal gifts; but we look
not so much as once towards him, nor will have him
to be our God.

. 72 .

God is not an angry God; if he were so we were
all utterly lost and undone. God does not willingly
strike mankind, except, as a just God, he be constrained thereunto; but, having no pleasure in un-
righteousness and ungodliness, he must therefore
suffer the punishment to go on. As I sometimes look
through the fingers, when the tutor whips my son
John, so it is with God; when we are unthankful
and disobedient to his word and commandments, he
suffers us, through the devil, to be soundly lashed
with pestilence, famine, and such like whips; not
that he is our enemy, and to destroy us, but that
through such scourging, he may call us to repentance and amendment, and so allure us to seek him,
run to him, and call upon him for help. Of this we
have a fine example in the book of Judges, where
the angel, in God's person, speaks thus: "I have
stricken you so often, and ye are nothing the better
for it;" and the people of Israel said: "Save thou
us but now; we have sinned and done amiss: punish

thou us, O Lord, and do with us what thou wilt, only save us now," &c. Whereupon he struck not all the people to death. In like manner did David, when he had sinned (in causing the people to be numbered, for which God punished the people with pestilence, so that 70,000 died), humble himself, saying: "Behold, Lord, I have sinned, I have done this misdeed, and have deserved this punishment: What have these sheep done? Let thy hand be upon me, and upon my father's house," &c. Then the Lord "repented him of the evil, and said to the angel that destroyed the people, It is enough, stay thy hand."

He that can humble himself earnestly before God in Christ, has already won; otherwise, the Lord God would lose his deity, whose own work it is, that he have mercy on the poor and sorrowful, and spare them that humble themselves before him. Were it not so, no human creature would come unto him, or call upon him; no man would be heard, no man saved, nor thank him; "For in hell no man praiseth thee," says the Psalm. The devil can affright, murder, and steal; but God revives and comforts.

This little word, God, is in the Scripture, a word with manifold significations, and is oftentimes understood of a thing after the nature of its operation and essence; as the devil is called a god; namely, a god of sin, of death, of despair, and damnation.

We must make due difference between this god and the upright and true God, who is a God of life, comfort, salvation, justification, and all goodness; for there are many words that bear no certain meanings, and equivocation is always the mother of error.

. 73 .

The wicked and ungodly enjoy the most part of God's creatures; the tyrants have the greatest power, lands, and people; the usurers the money; the farmers eggs, butter, corn, barley, oats, apples, pears, &c.; while godly Christians must suffer, be persecuted, sit in dungeons, where they can see neither sun nor moon, be thrust out into poverty, be banished, plagued, &c. But things will be better one day; they cannot always remain as now; let us have patience, and steadfastly remain by the pure doctrine, and not fall away from it, notwithstanding all this misery.

. 74 .

Our Lord God and the devil have two modes of policy which agree not together, but are quite opposite the one to the other. God at the first affrights, and afterwards lifts up and comforts again; so that the flesh and the old man should be killed, and the spirit, or new man, live. Whereas the devil makes, at first, people secure and bold, that they, void of all fear, may commit sin and wickedness, and not only remain in sin, but take delight and pleasure therein, and think they have done all well; but at last, when Mr. Stretch-leg comes, then he affrights and scares them without measure, so that they either die of great grief, or else, in the end, are left without all comfort, and despair of God's grace and mercy.

· 75 ·

God only, and not wealth, maintains the world; riches merely make people proud and lazy. At Venice, where the richest people are, a horrible dearth fell among them in our time, so that they were driven to call upon the Turks for help, who sent twenty-four galleys laden with corn; all which, well nigh in port, sunk before their eyes. Great wealth and money cannot still hunger, but rather occasion more dearth; for where rich people are, there things are always dear. Moreover, money makes no man right merry, but much rather pensive and full of sorrow; for riches, says Christ, are thorns that prick people. Yet is the world so mad that it sets therein all its joy and felicity.

· 76 ·

There is no greater anger than when God is silent, and talks not with us, but suffers us to go on in our sinful works, and to do all things according to our own passions and pleasure; as it has been with the Jews for the last fifteen hundred years.

Ah, God, punish, we pray thee, with pestilence and famine, and with what evil and sickness may be else on earth; but be not silent, Lord, towards us. God said to the Jews: "I have stretched forth mine hand, and have cried, come hither and hear," &c. "But ye said, We will not hear."

Even so likewise do we now; we are weary of God's word; we will not have upright, good, and godly preachers and teachers that threaten us, and bring God's word pure and unfalsified before us, and condemn false doctrine, and truly warn us. No, such cannot we endure; we will not hear them, nay, we persecute and banish them; therefore will God also punish us. Thus it goes with wicked and lost

children, that will not hearken to their parents, nor
be obedient unto them; they will afterwards be rejected of them again.

· 77 ·

Nothing displeases Almighty God more than
when we defend and cloak our sins, and will not
acknowledge that we have done wrong, as did Saul;
for the sins that be not acknowledged, are against
the first table of the Ten Commandments. Saul
sinned against the first table, David against the
second. Those are sinners against the second table,
that look on the sermon of Repentance, suffer themselves to be threatened and reproved, acknowledge
their sins, and better themselves. Those that sin
against the first table, as idolaters, unbelievers, contemners, and blasphemers of God, falsifiers of God's
word, &c. attribute to themselves wisdom and
power; they will be wise and mighty, both which
qualities God reserves to himself as peculiarly his
own.

· 78 ·

'Tis inexpressible how ungodly and wicked the
world is. We may easily perceive it from this, that
God has not only suffered punishments to increase,

but also has appointed so many executioners and hangmen to punish his subjects; as evil spirits, tyrants, disobedient children, knaves, and wicked women, wild beasts, vermin, sickness, &c.; yet all this can make us neither bend nor bow.

Better it were that God should be angry with us, than that we be angry with God, for he can soon be at an union with us again, because he is merciful; but when we are angry with him, then the case is not to be helped.

· 79 ·

God could be exceeding rich in temporal wealth, if he so pleased, but he will not. If he would but come to the pope, the emperor, a king, a prince, a bishop, a rich merchant, a citizen, a farmer, and say: Unless you give me a hundred thousand crowns, you shall die on the spot; every one would say: I will give it, with all my heart, if I may but live. But now we are such unthankful slovens, that we give him not so much as a *Deo gratias*, though we receive of him, to rich overflowing, such great benefits, merely out of his goodness and mercy. Is not this a shame? Yet, notwithstanding such un-thankfulness, our Lord God and merciful Father suffers not himself to be scared away, but continu-

ally shows us all manner of goodness. If in his gifts
and benefits he were more sparing and close-handed,
we should learn to be thankful. If he caused every
human creature to be born but with one leg or foot,
and seven years afterwards gave him the other;
or in the fourteenth year gave one hand, and afterwards, in the twentieth year, the other, then we
should better acknowledge God's gifts and benefits,
and value them at a higher rate, and be thankful.
He has given unto us a whole sea-full of his Word,
all manner of languages and liberal arts. We buy at
this time, cheaply, all manner of good books. He
gives us learned people, that teach well and regularly, so that a youth, if he be not altogether a dunce,
may learn more in one year now, than formerly in
many years. Arts are now so cheap, that almost
they go about begging for bread; woe be to us
that we are so lazy, improvident, negligent, and
unthankful.

· 80 ·

We are nothing worth with all our gifts and qualities, how great soever they be, unless God continually hold his hand over us: if he forsake us,
then are our wisdom, art, sense, and understanding
futile. If he do not constantly aid us, then our high-

est knowledge and experience in divinity, or what else we attain unto, will nothing serve; for when the hour of trial and temptation comes, we shall be despatched in a moment, the devil, through his craft and subtilty, tearing away from us even those texts in Holy Scriptures wherewith we should comfort ourselves, and setting before our eyes, instead, only sentences of fearful threatening.

Wherefore, let no man proudly boast and brag of his own righteousness, wisdom, or other gifts and qualities, but humble himself, and pray with the holy apostles, and say: Ah, Lord! strengthen and increase the faith in us!

· 81 ·

The greater God's gifts and works, the less are they regarded. The highest and most precious treasure we receive of God is, that we can speak, hear, see, &c.; but how few acknowledge these as God's special gifts, much less give God thanks for them. The world highly esteems riches, honour, power, and other things of less value, which soon vanish away, but a blind man, if in his right wits, would willingly exchange all these for sight. The reason why the corporal gifts of God are so much undervalued is, that they are so common, that God be-

stows them also upon brute beasts, which as well as
we, and better, hear and see. Nay, when Christ made
the blind to see, drove out devils, raised the dead,
&c., he was upbraided by the ungodly hypocrites,
who gave themselves out for God's people, and was
told that he was a Samaritan, and had a devil. Ah!
the world is the devil's whether it goes or stands
still; how, then, can men acknowledge God's gifts
and benefits? It is with us as with young children,
who regard not so much their daily bread, as an
apple, a pear, or other toys. Look at the cattle going
into the fields to pasture, and behold in them our
preachers, our milk-bearers, butter-bearers, cheese
and wool-bearers, which daily preach unto us faith
in God, and that we should trust in him, as in our
loving Father, who cares for us, and will maintain
and nourish us.

· 82 ·

No man can estimate the great charge God is at
only in maintaining birds and such creatures, comparatively nothing worth. I am persuaded that it
costs him, yearly, more to maintain only the spar-
rows, than the revenue of the French king amounts
to. What, then, shall we say of all the rest of his
creatures?

· 83 ·

God delights in our temptations, and yet hates
them; he delights in them when they drive us to
prayer: he hates them when they drive us to despair. The Psalm says: An humble and contrite
heart is an acceptable sacrifice to God, &c. Therefore, when it goes well with you, sing and praise
God with a hymn: goes it evil, that is, does temptation come, then pray: "For the Lord has pleasure
in those that fear him;" and that which follows is
better: "and in them that hope in his goodness:"
for God helps the lowly and humble, seeing he says:
"Thinkest thou my hand is shortened, that I cannot
help?" He that feels himself weak in faith, let him
always have a desire to be strong therein, for that
is a nourishment which God relishes in us.

· 84 ·

God, in this world, has scarce the tenth part of
the people; the smallest number only will be saved.
The world is exceedingly ungodly and wicked; who
would believe our people should be so unthankful
towards the gospel?

· 85 ·

'Tis wonderful how God has put such excellent

physic in mere muck; we know by experience that swine's dung stints the blood; horse's serves for the pleurisy; man's heals wounds and black blotches; asses' is used for the bloody flux, and cow's, with preserved roses, serves for epilepsy, or for convulsions of children.

· 86 ·

God seems as though he had dealt inconsiderately in commanding the world to be governed by the Word of Truth, especially since he has clothed and hooded it with a poor, weak, and contemned Word of the Cross. For, the world will not have the truth, but lies; neither willingly do they aught that is upright and good, unless compelled thereto by main force. The world has a loathing of the cross, and will rather follow the pleasures of the devil, and have pleasant days, than carry the cross of our blessed Saviour Christ Jesus. He that best governs the world, as most worthy of it, is Satan, by his lieutenant the pope; he can please the world well, and knows how to make it give ear unto him; for his kingdom has a mighty show and repute, which is acceptable to the world, and befits it. Like unto like.

· 87 ·

Pythagoras, the heathen philosopher, said, that
the motion of the stars creates a very sweet harmony and celestial concord; but that people,
through continual custom, have become cloyed
therewith. Even so it is with us; we have surpassing
fair creatures to our use, but by reason they are
too common, we regard them not.

· 88 ·

Scarcely a small proportion of the earth bears
corn, and yet we are all maintained and nourished.
I verily believe that there grow not as many sheaves
of corn as there are people in the world, and yet
we are all fed; yea, and there remains a good sur-
plus of corn at the year's end. This is a wonderful
thing, which should make us see and perceive God's
blessing.

· 89 ·

It is often asked: Why desperate wretches have
such good days, and live a long time in jollity and
pleasure, to their heart's desire, with health of body,
fine children, &c., while God allows the godly to remain in calamity, danger, anguish and want all

their lives; yea, and some to die also in misery, as St. John the Baptist did, who was the greatest saint on earth, to say nothing of our only Saviour Jesus Christ.

The prophets have all written much hereof, and shown how the godly should overcome such doubts, and comfort themselves against them. Jeremiah says, "Why goeth it so well with the ungodly, and wherefore are all they happy that deal very treacherously?" But further on, "Thou sufferest them to go at liberty like sheep that are to be slain, and thou preparest them for the day of slaughter." Read also Psalms xxxvii., xlix, lxxiii.

God is not therefore angry with his children, though he scourge and punish them; but he is angry with the ungodly that do not acknowledge Christ to be the Son of God, and the Saviour of the world, but blaspheme and contemn the Word; such are to expect no grace and help of him. And, indeed, he does not himself scourge and beat his small and poor flock that depend on Christ; but suffers them to be chastened and beaten, when they become oversecure and unthankful unto him for his unspeakable graces and benefits shown unto them in Christ, and are disobedient to his word; then permits he that the devil bruise our heels, and send pestilence

and other plagues unto us; and that tyrants persecute us, and this for our good, that thereby we
may be moved, and in a manner forced to turn ourselves unto him, to call upon him, to seek help and
comfort from him, through Christ.

· 90 ·

"God is a God of the living, and not of the dead."
This text shows the resurrection; for if there were
no hope of the resurrection, or of another and
better world, after this short and miserable life,
wherefore should God offer himself to be our God,
and say he will give us all that is necessary and
healthful for us, and, in the end, deliver us out of
all trouble, both temporal and spiritual? To what
purpose should we hear his Word, and believe in
him? What were we the better when we cry and
sigh to him in our anguish and need, that we wait
with patience upon his comfort and salvation, upon
his grace and benefits, shown in Christ? Why praise
and thank him for them? Why be daily in danger,
and suffer ourselves to be persecuted and slain for
the sake of Christ's Word?

Forasmuch as the everlasting, merciful God,
through his Word and Sacraments, talks and deals
with us, all other creatures excluded, not of tem-

poral things which pertain to this vanishing life,
and which in the beginning he provided richly for
us, but as to where we shall go when we depart
hence, and gives unto us his Son for a Saviour,
delivering us from sin and death, and purchasing
for us everlasting righteousness, life, and salvation,
therefore it is most certain, that we do not die away
like the beasts that have no understanding; but so
many of us as sleep in Christ, shall through him
be raised again to life everlasting at the last day,
and the ungodly to everlasting destruction. (John,
v., Dan. xii.)

· 91 ·

The most acceptable service we can do and show
unto God, and which alone he desires of us, is, that
he be praised of us; but he is not praised, unless he
be first loved; he is not loved, unless he be first
bountiful and does well; he does well when he is
gracious; gracious he is when he forgives sins. Now
who are those that love him? They are that small
flock of the faithful, who acknowledge such graces,
and know that through Christ they have forgiveness
of their sins. But the children of this world do
not trouble themselves herewith; they serve their

idol, that wicked and cursed Mammon: in the end
he will reward them.

· 92 ·

Our loving Lord God wills that we eat, drink, and
be merry, making use of his creatures, for therefore
he created them. He will not that we complain, as
if he had not given sufficient, or that he could not
maintain our poor carcases; he asks only that we
acknowledge him for our God, and thank him for
his gifts.

· 93 ·

He that has not God, let him have else what he
will, is more miserable than Lazarus, who lay at
the rich man's gate, and was starved to death. It
will go with such, as it went with the glutton, that
they must everlastingly hunger and want, and shall
not have in their power so much as one drop of
water.

· 94 ·

Of Abraham came Isaac and Ishmael; of the
patriarchs and holy fathers, came the Jews that
crucified Christ; of the apostles came Judas the

traitor; of the city Alexandria (where a fair, il-
lustrious, and famous school was, and whence proceeded many upright and godly learned men) came
Arius and Origen; of the Roman church, that
yielded many holy martyrs, came the blasphemous
Antichrist, the pope of Rome; of the holy men in
Arabia, came Mohammad; of Constantinople, where
many excellent emperors were, came the Turk; of
married women come adulteresses; of virgins,
strumpets; of brethren, sons, and friends, come
the cruelest enemies; of angels come devils; of kings
come tyrants; of the gospel and godly truth come
horrible lies; of the true church come heretics; of
Luther come fanatics, rebels, and enthusiasts. What
wonder is it then that evil is among us, comes from
us, and goes out of us; they must, indeed, be very
evil things that cannot stay by such goodness; and
they must also be very good, that can endure such
evil things.

· 95 ·

Though by reason of original sin many wild
beasts hurt mankind, as lions, wolves, bears, snakes.
adders, &c., yet the merciful God has in such manner mitigated our well-deserved punishments, that
there are many more beasts that serve us for our

good and profit, than of those which do us hurt:
many more sheep than wolves, oxen than lions, cows
than bears, deer than foxes, lobsters than scorpions,
ducks, geese, and hens, than ravens and kites, &c.:
in all creatures more good than evil, more benefits
than hurts and hindrances.

· 96 ·

The Scriptures show two manner of sacrifices acceptable to God. The first is called a sacrifice of
thanks or praise, and is when we teach and preach
God's Word purely, when we hear and receive it with
faith, when we acknowledge it, and do everything
that tends to the spreading of it abroad, and thank
God from our hearts for the unspeakable benefits
which through it are laid before us, and bestowed
upon us in Christ, when we praise and glorify him,
&c. "Offer unto God thanksgiving." "He that offereth
thanks praiseth me." "Thank the Lord, for he is
gracious, because his mercy endureth for ever."
"Praise the Lord, O my soul, and all that is within
me praise his holy name. Praise the Lord, O my
soul, and forget not all his benefits."—Psalms.

Secondly, when a sorrowful and troubled heart in
all manner of temptations has his refuge in God,
calls upon him in a true and upright faith, seeks

help of him, and waits patiently upon him. Hereof
the Psalms, "In my trouble I called upon the Lord,
and he heard me at large." "The Lord is nigh unto
them that are of a contrite heart, and will save such
as be of an humble spirit." "The sacrifice of God
is a troubled spirit; a broken and contrite heart, O
God, shalt thou not despise." And again: "Call upon
me in the time of need, so will I deliver thee, and
thou shalt praise me."

· 97 ·

If Adam had remained in his innocence, and had
not transgressed God's command, yet had begotten
children, he should not have lived and remained
continually in that state in Paradise, but would
have been taken into the everlasting glory of heaven,
not through death, but through being translated into
another life.

· 98 ·

God scorns and mocks the devil, in setting under
his very nose a poor, weak, human creature, mere
dust and ashes, yet endowed with the first-fruits of
the Spirit, against whom the devil can do nothing,
though he is so proud, subtile, and powerful a spirit.
We read in histories that a powerful king of Persia,

besieging the city of Edessa, the bishop, seeing that all human aid was ineffectual, and that the city could not of itself hold out, ascended to the ramparts and prayed to God, making, at the same time, the sign of the cross, whereupon there was a wonderful host sent from God of great flies and gnats, which filled the horses' eyes, and dispersed the whole army. Even so God takes pleasure to triumph and overcome, not through power, but by weakness.

· 99 ·

False teachers and sectaries are punishments for evil times, God's greatest anger and displeasure; while godly teachers are glorious witnesses, God's graces and mercies. Hence St. Paul names apostles, evangelists, prophets, shepherds, teachers, &c., gifts and presents of our Saviour Christ, sitting at the right hand of the Father. And the prophet Micah compares teachers of the gospel to a fruitful rain.

· 100 ·

Melancthon asked Luther if this word, hardened, "hardeneth whom he will," were to be understood directly as it sounded, or in a figurative sense? Luther answered: We must understand it specially and not operatively: for God works no evil. Through

his almighty power he works all in all; and as he
finds a man, so he works in him, as he did in
Pharaoh, who was evil by nature, which was not
God's, but his own fault; he continually went on in
his wickedness, doing evil; he was hardened, because God with his spirit and grace hindered not
his ungodly proceedings, but suffered him to go on,
and to have his way. Why God did not hinder or
restrain him, we ought not to inquire.

· 101 ·

God styles himself, in all the Holy Scriptures, a
God of life, of peace, of comfort, and joy, for the
sake of Christ. I hate myself, that I cannot believe
it so constantly and surely as I should; but no
human creature can rightly know how mercifully
God is inclined toward those that steadfastly believe in Christ.

· 102 ·

The second Psalm is one of the best Psalms. I
love that Psalm with my heart. It strikes and flashes
valiantly amongst kings, princes, counsellors,
judges, &c. If what this Psalm says be true, then
are the allegations and aims of the papists stark

lies and folly. If I were as our Lord God, and had committed the government to my son, as he to his Son, and these vile people were as disobedient as they now be, I would knock the world in pieces.

· 103 ·

If a man serve not God only, then surely he serves the devil; because no man can serve God, unless he have his Word and command. Therefore, if his Word and command be not in thy heart, thou servest not God, but thine own will; for that is upright serving of God, when a man does that which in his Word God has commanded to be done, every one in his vocation, not that which he thinks good of his own judgment.

· 104 ·

It troubles the hearts of people not a little, that God seems as though he were mutable or fickle-minded; for he gave to Adam the promise and cere-monies, which afterwards he altered with the rain-bow and the ark of Noah. He gave to Abraham the circumcision, to Moses he gave miraculous signs, to his people, the law. But to Christ, and through Christ, he gave the Gospel, which amounts to the abolition of all the former. Hence the Turks take advantage of these proceedings of God, saying: The laws of the Christians may be established, and endure for a time, but at last they will be altered.

· 105 ·

I was once sharply reprimanded by a popish priest, because, with such passion and vehemence, I reproved the people. I answered him: Our Lord God must first send a sharp, pouring shower, with thunder and lightning, and afterwards cause it mildly to rain, as then it wets finely through. I can easily cut a willow or a hazel wand with my trencher-knife, but for a hard oak, a man must use the axe; and little enough, to fell and cleave it.

· 106 ·

Plato, the heathen, said of God: God is nothing and yet everything; him followed Eck and the sophists, who understood nothing thereof, as their words show. But we must understand and speak of it in this manner: God is incomprehensible and invisible; that, therefore, which may be seen and comprehended, is not God. And thus, in another

manner, God is visible and invisible: visible in his
word and works; and where his word and works
are not, there a man should not desire to have him;
or he will, instead of God, take hold of the devil.
Let us not flutter too high, but remain by the manger and the swaddling clothes of Christ, "in whom
dwelleth all the fulness of the Godhead bodily."
There a man cannot fail of God, but finds him most
certainly. Human comfort and divine comfort are
of different natures: human comfort consists in external, visible help, which a man may see, hold,
and feel; divine comfort only in words and promises, where there is neither seeing, hearing, nor
feeling.

· 107 ·

When we see no way or means, by advice or aid,
through which we may be helped in our miseries,
we at once conclude, according to our human reason: now our condition is desperate; but when we
believe trustingly in God, our deliverance begins
The physician says: Where philosophy ends, physic
begins; so we say: Where human help is at an end,
God's help begins, or faith in God's word. Trials
and temptations appear before deliverance, after

deliverance comes joy. To be suppressed and troubled, is to arise, to grow and to increase.

· 108 ·

The devil, too, has his amusement and pleasure, which consists in suppressing God's work, and tormenting those that love God's word, and hold fast thereby; so the true Christians, being God's kingdom, must be tormented and oppressed.

A true Christian must have evil days, and suffer much; our Adam's flesh and blood must have good and easy days, and suffer nothing. How may these agree together? Our flesh is given over to death and hell: if our flesh is to be delivered from death, hell, and the devil, it must keep and hold to God's commandments—i. e., must believe in Christ Jesus, that he is the Son of God and our Redeemer, and must cleave fast to his word, believing that he will not suffer us to be plagued everlastingly, but will deliver and remove us out of this life into life eternal; giving us, at the same time, patience under the cross, and to bear with the weakness of another, who is also under the cross, and holds with Christ.

Therefore, he that will boast himself to be Christ's disciple, a true Christian, and saved, must not expect good days; but all his faith, hope and love must be directed to God, and to his neighbour, that so his whole life be nothing else than the cross, persecution, adversity, and tribulation.

· 109 ·

I would give a world to have the acts and legends of the patriarchs who lived before the deluge; for therein a man might see how they lived, preached, and what they suffered. But it pleased our Lord God to overwhelm all their acts and legends in the deluge, because he knew that those which should come after, would not regard, much less understand them; therefore God would keep and preserve them until they met again together in the life to come. But then, I am sure, the loving patriarchs who lived after the deluge, Abraham, Isaac, Jacob, &c.; the prophets, the apostles, their posterity, and other holy people, whom in this life the devil would not leave untempted, will yield unto the patriarchs, that lived before the deluge, and give to them preeminence in divine and spiritual honour, saying: Ye loving and most venerable patriarchs! I preached but a few years, spreading God's word abroad, and therefore suffered the cross; but what is that in comparison with the great, tedious, intolerable labour and pains, anguish, torments, and plagues, which ye, holy fathers, endured before the deluge, some of you, seven hundred, some eight hundred years, some longer, of the devil and the wicked world.

· 110 ·

As lately I lay very sick, so sick that I thought I should have left this world, many cogitations and musings had I in my weakness. Ah! thought I, what may eternity be? What joys may it have? However, I know for certain, that this eternity is ours; through Christ it is given and prepared for us, if we can but believe. There it shall be opened and revealed; here we shall not know when a second creation of the world will be, seeing we understand not the first. If I had been with God Almighty before he created the world, I could not have advised him how out of nothing to make this globe, the firmament, and that glorious sun, which in its swift course gives light to the whole earth; how, in such manner, to create man and woman, &c., all which he did for us, without our counsel. Therefore ought we justly to give him the honour, and leave to his divine power and goodness the new creation of the life to come, and not presume to speculate thereon.

· 111 ·

I hold that the name Paradise applies to the whole world. Moses describes more particularly what fell within Adam's sight before his fall—a sweet and pleasant place, watered by four rivers. After he had sinned, he directed his steps towards Syria, and the earth lost its fertility. Samaria and Judea were once fruitful lands, worthy to be Paradise, but they are now arid sand, for God has cursed them.

Even so, in our time, has God cursed fruitful lands, and caused them to be barren and unfruitful by reason of our sins, for where God gives not his blessing, there grows nothing that is good and profitable, but where he blesses, there all things grow plentifully, and are fruitful.

· 112 ·

Dr. Jonas, inviting Luther to dinner, caused a bunch of ripe cherries to be hung over the table where they dined, in remembrance of the creation, and as a suggestion to his guests to praise God for creating such fruits. But Luther said: Why not rather remember this in one's children, that are the fruit of one's body? For these are far more excelling creatures of God than all the fruits of trees. In them we see God's power, wisdom, and art, who made them all out of nothing, gave them life and limbs, exquisitely constructed, and will maintain and preserve them. Yet how little do we regard this. When people have children, all the effect is to make them grasping, raking together all they can to leave behind them. They do not know, that before a child comes into the world, it has its lot assigned already, and that it is ordained and determined what and how much it shall have. In the married state we find that the conception of children depends not on our will and pleasure; we never know whether we shall be fruitful or no, or whether God will give us a son or a daughter. All this goes on without our counsel. My father and mother did not imagine they should have brought a spiritual overseer into the world. 'Tis God's work only, and this we cannot enter into. I believe that, in the life to come, we shall have nothing to do, but to meditate on and marvel at our Creator and his creatures.

· 113 ·

A comet is a star that runs, not being fixed like a planet, but a bastard among planets. It is a haughty and proud star, engrossing the whole element, and carrying itself as if it were there alone. 'Tis of the nature of heretics, who also will be singular and alone, bragging and boasting above others, and thinking they are the only people endued with understanding.

· 114 ·

Whereto serve or profit such superfluity, such show, such ostentation, such extraordinarily luxurious kind of life as is now come upon us. If Adam were to return to earth, and see our mode of living, our food, drink, and dress, how would he marvel. He would say: Surely, this is not the world I was in; it was, doubtless, another Adam than I, who appeared among men heretofore. For Adam drank water, ate fruit from the trees, and, if he had any house at all, 'twas a hut, supported by four wooden forks; he had no knife, or iron; and he wore simply a coat of skin. Now we spend immense sums in eating and drinking; now we raise sumptuous palaces, and decorate them with a luxury beyond all comparison. The ancient Israelites lived in great moderation and quiet; Boaz says: "Dip thy bread in vinegar, and refresh thyself therewith." Judea was full of people, as we read in the book of Joshua; and a great multitude of people gives a lesson to live sparingly.

· 115 ·

Adam, our father, was, doubtless, a most miserable, plagued man. 'Twas a mighty solitariness for him to be alone in so wide and vast a world; but when he, with Eve, his only companion and loving consort, obtained Cain their son, then there was great joy, and so, when Abel was born; but soon after followed great trouble, misery, and sorrow of heart, when one brother slew another, and Adam thereby lost one son, and the other was banished and proscribed from his sight. This surely was a great cross and sorrow, so that the murder caused him more grief than his own fall; but he, with his loving Eve, were reduced again to a solitary kind of life. Afterwards, when he was one hundred and thirty years old, he had Seth. Miserable and lamentable was his fall, for during nine hundred years he saw God's anger in the death of every human creature. Ah! no human creature can conceive his perplexities: our sufferings, in comparison with his, are altogether children's toys; but he was afterwards comforted and refreshed again with the promise, through faith, of the woman's seed.

· 116 ·

All wild beasts are beasts of the law, for they live

in fear and quaking; they have all swarthy and
black flesh, by reason of their fear, but tame beasts
have white flesh, for they are beasts of grace; they
live securely with mankind.

· 117 ·

After Adam had lost the righteousness in which
God had created him, he was, without doubt, much
decayed in bodily strength, by reason of his anguish
and sorrow of heart. I believe that before the fall
he could have seen objects a hundred miles off better than we can see them at half a mile, and so in
proportion with all the other senses. No doubt,
after the fall, he said: "Ah, God! what has befallen
me? I am both blind and deaf." It was a horrible
fall; for, before, all creatures were obedient unto
him, so that he could play even with the serpent.

· 118 ·

Twenty years is but a short time, yet in that short
time the world were empty, if there was no marrying and production of children. God assembles unto
himself a Christian church out of little children.
For I believe, when a little child dies of one year
old, that always one, yea, two thousand die with it,
of that age or younger; but when I, Luther, die,

that am sixty-three, I believe that not three-score, or one hundred at the most, will die with me of that age, or older; for people now grow not old; not many people live to my years. Mankind is nothing else but a sheep-shambles, where we are slain and slaughtered by the devil. How many sorts of deaths are in our bodies? Nothing is therein but death.

· 119 ·

It is in the father's power to disinherit a disobedient child; God commanded, by Moses, that disobedient children should be stoned to death, so that a father may clearly disinherit a son, yet with this proviso, that, upon bettering and amendment, he reinstate him.

· 120 ·

What need had our early ancestors of other food than fruits and herbs, seeing these tasted so well and gave such strength? The pomegranates and oranges, without doubt, yielded such a sweet and pleasant smell, that one might have been satisfied with the scent thereof; and I am sure Adam, before his fall, never wanted to eat a partridge; but the deluge spoiled all. It follows not, that because God created all things, we must eat of all things. Fruits were created chiefly as food for people and for beasts; the latter were created to the end we should laud and praise God. Whereunto serve the stars, but only to praise their Creator? Whereunto serve the raven and crows, but to call upon the Lord who nourishes them.

· 121 ·

There's no doubt that all created things have degenerated by reason of original sin. The serpent was at first a lofty, noble animal, eating without fear from Eve's hand, but after it was cursed, it lost its feet, and was fain to crawl and eat on the ground. It was precisely because the serpent, at that time, was the most beautiful of creatures, that Satan selected it for his work, for the devil likes beauty, knowing that beauty attracts men unto evil. A fool serves not as a provocative to heresy, nor a deformed maid-servant to libertinism, nor water to drunkenness, nor rags to vanity. Consider the bodies of children, how much sweeter and purer and more beautiful they are than those of grown persons; 'tis because childhood approaches nearer to the state of innocence wherein Adam lived before his fall. In our sad condition, our only consolation is

the expectation of another life. Here below all is
incomprehensible.

· 122 ·

Dr. Luther, holding a rose in his hand, said: 'Tis
a magnificent work of God: could a man make but
one such rose as this, he would be thought worthy
of all honour, but the gifts of God lose their value
in our eyes, from their very infinity. How wonderful is the resemblance between children and their
parents. A man shall have half-a-dozen sons, all
like him as so many peas are like another, and
these sons again their sons, with equal exactness
of resemblance, and so it goes on. The heathen
noticed these likenesses. Dido says to Æneas:

"Si mihi parvulus Æneas luderet in aulâ,
Qui te tantum ore referret."

'Twas a form of malediction among the Greeks, for
a man to wish that his enemy's son might be unlike
him in face.

· 123 ·

'Tis wonderful how completely the earth is fer-
tilized by currents of water running in all directions
and constantly replenished by snow, rain, and dew.

OF THE NATURE
OF THE WORLD

· 124 ·

HE that is now a prince, wants to be a king or an emperor. A man in love with a girl is ever casting about how he may come to marry her, and in his eyes there is none fairer than she; when he has got her, he is soon weary of her, and thinks another more fair, whom easily he might have had. The poor man thinks, had I but twenty pounds I should be rich enough; but when he has got that, he would have more. The heart is inconsistent in all things, as the heathen says: *Virtutem præsentem odimus, sublatam ex oculis quærimus invidi.*

· 125 ·

One knife cuts better than another; so, likewise, one that has learned languages and arts can better and more distinctly teach than another. But in that many of them, as Erasmus and others, are well versed in languages and arts, and yet err with great hurt, 'tis as with the greater sort of weapons, which are made to kill: we must distinguish the thing from the abuse.

· 126 ·

The wickedness of the enemies of the Word is not human, but altogether devilish. A human creature is wicked according to the manner and nature of mankind, and according as he is spoiled through original sin, but when he is possessed and driven of the devil, then begins the most bitter and cruel combat between him and the woman's seed.

· 127 ·

The world will neither hold God for God, nor the devil for the devil. And if a man were left to himself, to do after his own kind and nature, he would willingly throw our Lord God out at the window; for the world regards God nothing at all, as the psalm says: The wicked man saith in his heart, there is no God.

· 128 ·

The god of the world is riches, pleasure, and pride, wherewith it abuses all the creatures and gifts of God.

· 129 ·

We have the nature and manner of all wild beasts in eating. The wolves eat sheep; we also. The foxes eat hens, geese, &c.; we also. The hawks and kites eat fowl and birds; we also. Pikes eat other fish; we also. With oxen, horse, and kine, we also eat salads, grass, &c.

· 130 ·

I much wonder how the heathen could write such fair and excellent things of death, seeing it is so grisly and fearful! But when I remember the nature of the world, then I wonder nothing at all; for they saw great evil and wickedness flourishing among them, and in their rulers, which sorely grieved them, and they had nothing else to threaten and terrify their rulers with, but death.

Now, if the heathen so little regarded death, nay, so highly and honourably esteemed it, how much more so ought we Christians? For they, poor people, knew less than nothing of the life eternal, while we know and are instructed in it; yet, when we only speak of death, we are all affrighted.

The cause hereof is our sins; we live worse than the heathen, and therefore cannot justly complain, for the greater our sins, the more fearful is death.

See those who have rejected God's word: when they are at the point of death, and are put in mind of the day of judgment, how fearfully do they tremble and shake.

· 131 ·

Here, to-day, have I been pestered with the knaveries and lies of a baker, brought before me for using false weights, though such matters concern the magistrate rather than the divine. Yet if no one were to check the thefts of these bakers, we should have a fine state of things.

· 132 ·

There is not a more dangerous evil than a flattering, dissembling counsellor. While he talks, his advice has hands and feet, but when it should be put in practice, it stands like a mule, which will not be spurred forward.

· 133 ·

There are three sorts of people: the first, the common sort, who live secure without remorse of conscience, acknowledging not their corrupt manners and natures, insensible of God's wrath against their sins, and careless thereof. The second, those who through the law are scared, feel God's anger, and strive and wrestle with despair. The third, those that acknowledge their sins and God's merited wrath, feel themselves conceived and born in sin, and therefore deserving of perdition, but, notwithstanding, attentively hearken to the gospel, and believe that God, out of grace, for the sake of Jesus Christ, forgives sins, and so are justified before God, and afterwards show the fruits of their faith by all manner of good works.

· 134 ·

That matrimony is matrimony, that the hand is a hand, that goods are goods, people well understand; but to believe that matrimony is God's creation and ordinance, that the hands, that the goods, as food and raiment, and other creatures we use, are given and presented unto us of God, 'tis God's special work and grace when men believe it.

· 135 ·

The heart of a human creature is like quicksilver, now here, now there; this day so, to-morrow otherwise. Therefore vanity is a poor miserable thing, as Ecclesiasticus says. A man desires and longs after things that are uncertain and of doubtful result, but contemns that which is certain, done, and accomplished. Therefore what God gives us we will not have; for which cause Christ would not govern on earth, but gave it over to the devil, saying, "Rule thou." God is of another nature, manner, and mind. I, he says, am God, and therefore change not; I hold fast and keep sure my promises and threatenings.

· 136 ·

He must be of a high and great spirit that undertakes to serve the people in body and soul, for he must suffer the utmost danger and unthankfulness. Therefore Christ said to Peter, Simon, &c., "Lovest thou me?" repeating it three times together. Then he said: "Feed my sheep," as if he would say, "Wilt thou be an upright minister, and a shepherd? then love must only do it, thy love to me; for how else could ye endure unthankfulness, and spend wealth and health, meeting only with persecution and ingratitude?"

· 137 ·

The highest wisdom of the world is to busy itself with temporal, earthly, and ephemeral things; and when these go ill, it says, Who would have thought

it? But faith is a certain and sure expectation of
that which a man hopes for, making no doubt of
that which yet he sees not. A true Christian does not
say: I had not thought it, but is most certain that
the beloved cross is near at hand; and thus is not
afraid when it goes ill with him, and he is tormented. But the world, and those who live secure
in it, cannot bear misfortune; they go on continually dancing in pleasure and delight, like the
rich glutton in the gospel. He could not spare the
scraps to poor Lazarus; but Lazarus belongs to
Christ, and will take his part with him.

· 138 ·

The world seems to me like a decayed house,
David and the prophets being the spars, and Christ
the main pillar in the midst, that supports all.

· 139 ·

As all people feel they must die, each seeks im-
mortality here on earth, that he may be had in
everlasting remembrance. Some great princes and
kings seek it by raising great columns of stone, and
high pyramids, great churches, costly and glorious
palaces, castles, &c. Soldiers hunt after praise and
honour, by obtaining famous victories. The learned

seek an everlasting name by writing books. With
these, and such like things, people think to be im-
mortal. But as to the true, everlasting, and incor-
ruptible honour and eternity of God, no man thinks
or looks after it. Ah! we are poor, silly, miserable
people!

. 140 .

To live openly among the people is best; Christ
so lived and walked, openly and publicly, here on
earth, amongst the people, and told his disciples to
do the like. 'Tis in cells and corners that the wicked
wretches, the monks and nuns, lead shameful lives.
But openly, and among people, a man must live
decently and honestly.

. 141 .

To comfort a sorrowful conscience is much better than to possess many kingdoms; yet the world
regards it not; nay, contemns it, calling us rebels,
disturbers of the peace, and blasphemers of God,
turning and altering religion. They will be their
own prophets, and prophesy to themselves; but this
to us is a great grief of heart. The Jews said of
Christ, If we suffer him to go on in this manner,

the Romans will come and take from us land and people. After they had slain Christ, did the Romans come or not? Yea, they came, and slew a hundred thousand of them, and destroyed their city. Even so the contemners and enemies of the Word will disturb the peace, and turn Germany upside down. We bring evil upon ourselves, for we wilfully oppose the truth.

· 142 ·

If Moses had continued to work his miracles in Egypt but two or three years, the people would have become accustomed thereto, and heedless, as we who are accustomed to the sun and moon, hold them in no esteem.

· 143 ·

Abraham was held in no honour among the Canaanites, for all the wells he had dug the neighbours filled up, or took away by force, and said to him: Wilt thou not suffer it? then pack thee hence and be gone, for thou art with us a stranger and a new comer. In like manner, Isaac was despised. The faith possessed by the beloved patriarchs, I am not able sufficiently to admire. How firmly and constantly did they believe that God was gracious unto them, though they suffered such exceeding trouble and adversity!

· 144 ·

If the great pains and labour I take sprang not from the love, and for the sake of him that died for me, the world could not give me money enough to write only one book, or to translate the Bible. I desire not to be rewarded and paid of the world for my books; the world is too poor to give me satisfaction; I have not asked the value of one penny of my master the Prince Elector of Saxony, since I have been here. The world is nothing but a reversed Decalogue, or the Ten Commandments backwards, a mask and picture of the devil, all contemners of God, all blasphemers, all disobedient; harlotry, pride, theft, murder, &c. are now almost ripe for the slaughter.

· 145 ·

Dr. Luther's wife complaining to him of the indocility and untrustworthiness of servants, he said: A faithful and good servant is a real God-send, but, truly, 'tis a *rare bird in the land*. We find every one complaining of the idleness and profligacy of this class of people; we must govern them, Turkish fashion, so much work, so much victuals, as Pharaoh dealt with the Israelites in Egypt.

· 146 ·

The philosophers, and learned among the heathen, had innumerable speculations as to God, the soul, and the life everlasting, all uncertain and doubtful, they being without God's Word; while to us, God has given his most sweet and saving Word, pure and incorrupt; yet we contemn it. It is naught, says the buyer. When we have a thing, how good soever, we are soon weary of it, and regard it not. The world remains the world, which neither loves nor endures righteousness, but is ruled by a certain few, even as a little boy of twelve years old rules, governs, and keeps a hundred great and strong oxen upon a pasture.

· 147 ·

Whoso relies on his money prospers not. The richest monarchs have had ill fortune, have been destroyed and slain in the wars; while men with but small store of money have had great fortune and victory; as the emperor Maximilian overcame the Venetians, and continued warring ten years with

them, though they were exceedingly rich and powerful. Therefore we ought not to trust in money or
wealth, or depend thereon. I hear that the prince
elector, George, begins to be covetous, which is a
sign of his death very shortly. When I saw Dr. Gode
begin to tell his puddings hanging in the chimney,
I told him he would not live long, and so it fell
out; and when I begin to trouble myself about
brewing, malting, cooking, &c., then shall I soon
die.

· 148 ·

We should always be ready when God knocks,
prepared to take our leave of this world like Christians. For even as the small beast kills the stag, leaping upon his head, and sitting between his horns,
and eating out his brains, or catches him fast by
the throat, and gnaws it asunder, even so the devil,
when he possesses a human creature, is not soon or
easily pulled from him, but leads him into despair,
and hurts him both in soul and body; as St. Peter
says: "He goeth about like a roaring lion."

· 149 ·

Before Noah's flood the world was highly learned,
by reason men lived a long time, and so attained

great experience and wisdom, now, ere we begin rightly to come to the true knowledge of a thing, we lie down and die. God will not have that we should attain a higher knowledge of things.

· 150 ·

Mammon has two properties; it makes us secure, first, when it goes well with us, and then we live without fear of God at all; secondly, when it goes ill with us, then we tempt God, fly from him, and seek after another God.

· 151 ·

I saw a dog, at Lintz, in Austria, that was taught to go with a hand-basket to the butchers' shambles for meat; when other dogs came about him, and sought to take the meat out of the basket, he set it down, and fought lustily with them; but when he saw they were too strong for him, he himself would snatch out the first piece of meat, lest he should lose all. Even so does now our emperor Charles; who, after having long protected spiritual benefices, seeing that every prince takes possession of monasteries, himself takes possession of bishoprics, as just now he has seized upon those of Utrecht and Liege.

· 152 ·

A man that depends on the riches and honours of this world, forgetting God and the welfare of his soul, is like a little child that holds a fair apple in the hand, of agreeable exterior, promising goodness, but within 'tis rotten and full of worms.

· 153 ·

Where great wealth is, there are also all manner of sins; for through wealth comes pride, through pride, dissension, through dissension, wars, through wars, poverty, through poverty, great distress and misery. Therefore, they that are rich, must yield a strict and great account; for to whom much is given, of him much will be required.

· 154 ·

Riches, understanding, beauty, are fair gifts of God, but we abuse them shamefully. Yet worldly wisdom and wit are evils, when the cause engaged in is evil, for no man will yield his own particular conceit; every one will be right. Much better is it that one be of a fair and comely complexion in the face, for the hard lesson, sickness, may come and take that away; but the self-conceited mind is not so soon brought to reason.

· 155 ·

Wealth is the smallest thing on earth, the least gift that God has bestowed on mankind. What is it in comparison with God's Word—what, in comparison with corporal gifts, as beauty, health, &c.? —nay, what is it to the gifts of the mind, as understanding, wisdom, &c.? Yet are men so eager after it, that no labour, pains, or risk is regarded in the acquisition of riches. Wealth has in it neither material, formal, efficient, nor final cause, nor anything else that is good; therefore our Lord God commonly gives riches to those from whom he withholds spiritual good.

· 156 ·

St. John says: "He that hath this world's goods, and seeth his brother have need, and shutteth up his bowels of compassion from him, how dwelleth the love of God in him?" And Christ: "He that desireth of thee, give to him"—that is, to him that needs and is in want; not to idle, lazy, wasteful fellows, who are commonly the greatest beggars, and who, though we give them much and often, are nothing helped thereby. Yet when one is truly poor, to him I will give with all my heart, according to my ability. And no man should forget the Scripture: "He that hath two coats, let him part with one;" meaning all manner of apparel that one has need of, according to his state and calling, as well for credit as for necessity. As also, by "the daily bread," is understood all maintenance necessary for the body.

· 157 ·

Lendest thou aught? so gettest thou it not again. Even if it be restored, it is not so soon as it ought to be restored, nor so well and good, and thou losest a friend thereby.

· 158 ·

Before I translated the New Testament out of the Greek, all longed after it; when it was done, their longing lasted scarce four weeks. Then they desired the Books of Moses; when I had translated these, they had enough thereof in a short time. After that, they would have the Psalms; of these they were soon weary, and desired other books. So will it be with the Book of Ecclesiasticus, which they now long for, and about which I have taken great pains. All is acceptable until our giddy brains be satisfied; afterwards we let things lie, and seek after new.

OF JESUS CHRIST

· 159 ·

THE feast we call *Annunciatio Mariæ,* when the angel came to Mary, and brought her the message from God, that she should conceive his Son, may be fitly called the "Feast of Christ's Humanity;" for then began our deliverance. The mystery of the humanity of Christ, that he sunk himself into our flesh, is beyond all human understanding.

· 160 ·

Christ lived three and thirty years, and went up thrice every year to Jerusalem, making ninety-nine times he went thither. If the pope could show that Christ had been but once at Rome, what a bragging and boasting would he make! Yet Jerusalem was destroyed to the ground.

· 161 ·

St. Paul teaches, that Christ was born, to the end he might restore and bring everything to the state

103

in which it was created at the beginning of the
world; that is, to bring us to the knowledge of ourselves and our Creator, that we might learn to know
who and what we have been, and who and what we
now are; namely, that we were created after God's
likeness, and afterwards, according to the likeness
of man; that we were the devil's vizard through
sin, utterly lost and destroyed; and that now we
may be delivered from sin again, and become pure,
justified, and saved.

· 162 ·

All the wisdom of the world is childish foolishness in comparison with the acknowledgment of
Christ. For what is more wonderful than the unspeakable mystery, that the Son of God, the image
of the eternal Father, took upon him the nature of
man. Doubtless, he helped his supposed father,
Joseph, to build houses; for Joseph was a carpenter.
What will they of Nazareth think at the day of judgment, when they shall see Christ sitting in his divine
majesty; surely they will be astonished, and say:
Lord, thou helpest build my house, how comest thou
now to this high honour?

When Jesus was born, doubtless, he cried and
wept like other children, and his mother tended him

as other mothers tend their children. As he grew up, he was submissive to his parents, and waited on them, and carried his supposed father's dinner to him, and when he came back, Mary, no doubt, often said: "My dear little Jesus, where hast thou been?" He that takes not offence at the simple, lowly, and mean course of the life of Christ, is endued with high divine art and wisdom; yea, has a special gift of God in the Holy Ghost. Let us ever bear in mind, that our blessed Saviour thus humbled and abased himself, yielding even to the contumelious death of the cross, for the comfort of us poor, miserable, and damned creatures.

· 163 ·

If the emperor should wash a beggar's feet, as the French king used to do on Maunday Thursday, and the emperor Charles yearly, how would such humility be extolled and praised! But though the Son of God, Lord of all emperors, kings, and princes, in the deepest measure humbled himself, even to the death of the cross, yet no man wonders thereat, except only the small heap of the faithful who acknowledge and worship him as their only Lord and Saviour. He abased himself, indeed, enough, when he was held to be the man most

despised, plagued, and smitten of God (Isaiah liii.),
and for our sakes underwent and suffered shame.

· 164 ·

We cannot vex the devil more than by teaching,
preaching, singing, and talking of Jesus. Therefore
I like it well, when with sounding voice we sing in
the church: *Et homo factus est; et verbum caro
factum est.* The devil cannot endure these words,
and flies away, for he well feels what is contained
therein. Oh, how happy a thing were it, did we find
as much joy in these words as the devil is affrighted
at them. But the world contemns God's words and
works, because they are delivered to them in a plain
and simple manner. Well, the good and godly are
not offended therewith, for they have regard to the
everlasting celestial treasure and wealth which
therein lies hid, and which is so precious and glorious, that the angels delight in beholding it. Some
there are who take offence, that now and then in the
pulpits we say: Christ was a carpenter's son, and
as a blasphemer and rebel, he was put on the cross,
and hanged between two malefactors.

But seeing we preach continually of this article,
and in our children's creed, say: That our Saviour

Christ suffered under Pontius Pilate, was crucified, dead, and buried, &c. for our sins, why, then, should we not say Christ was a carpenter's son? especially seeing that he is clearly so named in the gospel, when the people wondered at his doctrine and wisdom, and said: How cometh this to pass? Is not this the carpenter, the son of Mary? (Mark, vi.)

· 165 ·

Sheb limini; that is, "Sit thou on my right hand." This *Sheb limini* has many and great enemies, whom we poor, small heap must endure; but 'tis no matter; many of us must suffer and be slain by their fury and rage, yet let us not be dismayed, but, with a divine resolution and courage, wage and venture ourselves, our bodies and souls, upon this his word and promise: "I live, and ye shall also live; and where I am, there shall ye be also."

Christ bears himself as though he took not the part of us his poor, troubled, persecuted members. For the world rewards God's best and truest servants very ill; persecuting, condemning, and killing them as heretics and malefactors, while Christ holds his peace and suffers it to be done, so that sometimes I have this thought: I know not where I am;

whether I preach right or no. This was also the temptation and trial of St. Paul, touching which he, however, spake not much, neither could, as I think; for who can tell what those words import: "I die daily."

The Scripture, in many places, calls Christ our priest, bridegroom, love's delight, &c., and us who believe in him, his bride, virgin, daughter, &c.; this is a fair, sweet, loving picture, which we always should have before our eyes. For, first, he has manifested his office of priesthood in this, that he has preached, made known, and revealed his Father's will unto us. Secondly, he has also prayed, and will pray for us true Christians so long as the world endures. Thirdly, he has offered up his body for our sins upon the cross. He is our bridegroom, and we are his bride. What he, the loving Saviour Christ has—yea himself, is ours; for we are members of his body, of his flesh and bone, as St. Paul says. And again, what we have, the same is also his; but the exchange is exceeding unequal; for he has everlasting innocence, righteousness, life, and salvation, which he gives to be our own, while what we have is sin, death, damnation, and hell; these we give unto him, for he has taken our sins upon

him, has delivered us from the power of the devil
and crushed his head, taken him prisoner, and cast
him down to hell; so that now we may, with St.
Paul, undauntedly say: "Death, where is thy sting?"
Yet, though our loving Saviour has solemnized this
spiritual wedding with us, and endued us with his
eternal, celestial treasure, and sworn to be our everlasting priest, yet the majority, in the devil's name,
run away from him, and worship strange idols, as
the Jews did, and as they in popedom do.

· 166 ·

"There is but one God," says St. Paul, "and one
mediator between God and man; namely, the man
Jesus Christ, who gave himself a ransom for all."
Therefore, let no man think to draw near unto God
or obtain grace of him, without this mediator, high-
priest, and advocate.

It follows that we cannot through our good works,
honesty of life, virtues, deserts, sanctity, or through
the works of the law, appease God's wrath, or obtain
forgiveness of sins; and that all deserts of saints are
quite rejected and condemned, so that through them
no human creature can be justified before God.
Moreover, we see how fierce God's anger is against
sins, seeing that by none other sacrifice or offering

could they be appeased and stilled, but by the precious blood of the Son of God.

· 167 ·

At Rome was a church called Pantheon, where were collected effigies of all the gods they were able to bring together out of the whole world. All these could well accord one with another, for the devil therewith jeered the world, laughing in his fist; but when Christ came, him they could not endure, but all the devils, idols, and heretics grew stark mad and full of rage; for he, the right and true God and man, threw them altogether on a heap. The pope also sets himself powerfully against Christ, but he must likewise be put to confusion and destroyed.

· 168 ·

The history of the resurrection of Christ, teaching that which human wit and wisdom of itself cannot believe, that "Christ is risen from the dead," was declared to the weaker and sillier creatures, women, and such as were perplexed and troubled.

Silly, indeed, before God, and before the world: first, before God, in that they "sought the living among the dead;" second, before the world, for they forgot the "great stone which lay at the mouth of the sepulchre," and prepared spices to anoint Christ, which was all in vain. But spiritually is hereby signified this: if the "great stone," namely, the law and human traditions, whereby the consciences are bound and snared, be not rolled away from the heart, then we cannot find Christ, or believe that he is risen from the dead. For through him we are delivered from the power of sin and death, Rom. viii., so that the hand-writing of the conscience can hurt us no more.

· 169 ·

Is it not a wonder beyond all wonders, that the Son of God, whom all angels and the heavenly hosts worship, and at whose presence the whole earth quakes and trembles, should have stood among those wicked wretches, and suffered himself to be so lamentably tormented, scorned, derided, and contemned? They spat in his face, struck him in the mouth with a reed, and said: O, he is a king, he must have a crown and a sceptre. The sweet blessed Saviour complains not in vain in the Psalm, *Diminuerunt omnia ossa mea*: now, if he suffered so much from the rage of men, what must he have felt when God's wrath was poured out upon him without measure? as St. Mark says: "He began to be sore amazed, and very heavy, and saith unto his disciples, My soul is exceeding sorrowful unto death:" and St. Luke says: "And being in an agony, he prayed more earnestly, and his sweat was as it were great drops of blood falling down to the ground." Ah! our suffering is not worthy the name of suffering. When I consider my crosses, tribulations, and temptations, I shame myself almost to death, thinking what are they in comparison of the sufferings of my blessed Saviour Christ Jesus. And yet we must be conformable to the express image of the Son of God. And what if we were conformable to the same, yet were it nothing. He is the Son of God, we are poor creatures; though we should suffer everlasting death, yet were they of no value.

· 170 ·

The conversation of Christ with his disciples, when he took his leave of them at his last supper, was most sweet, loving, and friendly, talking with them lovingly, as a father with his children, when he must depart from them. He took their weakness in good part, and bore with them, though now and then their discourse was very full of simplicity; as when Philip said: "Show us the Father," &c. And

Thomas: "We know not the way," &c. And Peter: "I will go with thee into death." Each freely showing the thoughts of his heart. Never, since the world began, was a more precious, sweet, and amiable conversation.

· 171 ·

Christ had neither money, nor riches, nor earthly kingdom, for he gave the same to kings and princes. But he reserved one thing peculiarly to himself, which no human creature or angel could do—namely, to conquer sin and death, the devil and hell, and in the midst of death to deliver and save those that through his word believe in him.

· 172 ·

The sweating of blood and other high spiritual sufferings that Christ endured in the garden, no human creature can know or imagine; if one of us should but begin to feel the least of those sufferings, he must die instantly. There are many who die of grief of mind; for sorrow of heart is death itself. If a man should feel such anguish and pain as Christ had, it were impossible for the soul to remain in the body and endure it—body and soul must part asunder. In Christ only it was possible, and from him issued bloody sweat.

· 173 ·

Nothing is more sure than this: he that does not take hold on Christ by faith, and comfort himself herein, that Christ is made a curse for him, remains under the curse. The more we labour by works to obtain grace, the less we know how to take hold on Christ; for where he is not known and comprehended by faith, there is not to be expected either advice, help, or comfort, though we torment ourselves to death.

· 174 ·

All the prophets well foresaw in the Spirit, that Christ, by imputation, would become the greatest sinner upon the face of the earth, and a sacrifice for the sins of the whole world; would be no more considered an innocent person and without sin, or the Son of God in glory, but a notorious sinner, and so be for awhile forsaken (Psal. viii.), and have lying upon his neck the sins of all mankind; the sins of St. Paul, who was a blasphemer of God, and a persecutor of his church; St. Peter's sins, that denied Christ; David's sins, who was an adul-

terer and a murderer, through whom the name of
the Lord among the heathen was blasphemed.

Therefore the law, which Moses gave to be executed upon all malefactors and murderers in general, took hold on Christ, finding him with and
among sinners and murderers, though in his own
person innocent.

This manner of picturing Christ to us, the sophists, robbers of God, obscure and falsify; for they
will not that Christ was made a curse for us, to the
end he might deliver us from the curse of the law,
nor that he has anything to do with sin and poor
sinners; though for their sakes alone was he made
man and died, but they set before use merely
Christ's examples, which they say we ought to imi-
tate and follow; and thus they not only steal from
Christ his proper name and title, but also make of
him a severe and angry judge, a fearful and horrible tyrant, full of wrath against poor sinners, and
bent on condemning them.

· 175 ·

The riding of our blessed Saviour into Jerusalem
was a poor, mean kind of procession enough, where
was seen Christ, king of heaven and earth, sitting
upon a strange ass, his saddle being the clothes of

his disciples. This mean equipage, for so powerful a potentate, was, as the prophecy of the prophet Zechariah showed, to the end the scripture might be fulfilled. Yet 'twas an exceeding stately and glorious thing as extolled through the prophecies, though outwardly to the world it seemed poor and mean.

I hold that Christ himself did not mention this prophecy, but that rather the apostles and evangelists used it for a witness. Christ, meantime, preached and wept, but the people honoured him with olive branches and palms, which are signs of peace and victory. Such ceremonies did the heathen receive of the Jews, and not the Jews of the heathen, as some pretend, for the nation of the Jews and Jerusalem was much older than the Greeks and Romans. The Greeks had their beginning about the time of the Babylonish captivity, but Jerusalem was long before the time of the Persians and Assyrians, and therefore much before the Greeks and Romans, so that the heathen received many ceremonies from the Jews, as the elder nation.

· 176 ·

The Jews crucified Christ with words, but the Gentiles have crucified him with works and deeds.

His sufferings were prophetical of our wickedness, for Christ suffers still to this day in our church much more than in the synagogue of the Jews; far greater blaspheming of God, contempt, and tyranny, is now among us than heretofore among the Jews. In Italy, when mention is made of the article of faith and of the last day of judgment, then says the pope with his greased crew: O! dost thou believe that? Pluck thou up a good heart, and be merry; let such cogitations alone. These and the like blasphemies are so common in all Italy, that, without fear of punishment, they openly proclaim them everywhere.

· 177 ·

The prophets spoke and preached of the second coming of Christ as we do now; we know that the last day will come, yet we know not what and how it will be after this life, but only in general, that we, who are true Christians, shall have everlasting joy, peace, and salvation. The prophets held likewise, that soon after the coming of Christ, the last day would appear. First, they named the day of the Messiah the last day. Secondly, they set the signs of the first and second coming both together, as if they would happen at one time. Thirdly, in the

Epistle to the Corinthians, they demanded of St. Paul, if the last day would appear while they lived. Fourthly, Christ himself related that these signs should come together. O! how willingly would I have been once with our Saviour Christ here on earth, when he rejoiced.

· 178 ·

My opinion is, that Christ descended into hell, to the end he might lay the devil in chains, in order to bring him to the judgment of the great day, as in the 16th Psalm, and Acts ii. Disputatious spirits allege, that the word *Infernus*, Hell, must be taken and understood to be the grave, as in the first book of Moses, but yet here is written not only the Hebrew word *Nabot*—that is, pit, but *Scola*—that is, *Gehenna*, Hell; for the ancients made four different hells.

· 179 ·

The communion or fellowship of our blessed Saviour Christ, was doubtless most loving and familiar; for he who thought it no dishonour, being equal with God, to be made man like unto us, yet without sin, served and waited upon his disciples as they sat at table, as my servant waits on me; the good disciples, plain, simple people, were at length so accustomed to it, that they were even content to let him wait. In such wise did Christ fulfil his office; as is written: "He is come to minister, and not to be ministered unto." Ah, 'tis a high example, that he so deeply humbled himself and suffered, who created the whole world, heaven and earth, and all that is therein, and who, with one finger, could have turned it upside down and destroyed it.

· 180 ·

How wonderfully does Christ rule and govern his kingdom, so concealing himself that his presence is not seen, yet putting to shame emperors, kings, popes, and all such as think themselves wise, just, and powerful. But hereunto belongs a *Plerophoria*—that is, we are sure and certain of it.

Jesus Christ is the only beginning and end of all my divine cogitations, day and night, yet I find and freely confess that I have attained but only to a small and weak beginning of the height, depth, and breadth of this immeasurable, incomprehensible, and endless wisdom, and have scarce got and

brought to light a few fragments out of this most
deep and precious profundity.

· 181 ·

Christ's own proper work and office is to combat
the law, sin, and death, for the whole world; taking
them all upon himself, and bearing them, and after
he has laden himself therewith, then only to get the
victory, and utterly overcome and destroy them,
and so release the desolate from the law and all
evil. That Christ expounds the law, and works
miracles, these are but small benefits, in comparison
of the true good, for which he chiefly came. For
the prophets, and especially the apostles, wrought
and did as great miracles as Christ himself.

· 182 ·

That our Saviour, Christ, is come, nothing avails
hypocrites, who live confident, not fearing God, nor
contemners nor reprobates, who think there is no
grace or comfort to be expected, and who by the
law are affrighted. But he comes to the profit and
comfort of those whom for a time the law has
plagued and affrighted; these despair not in their
trials and affrights, but with comfortable confidence

step to Christ, the throne of grace, who delivers them.

· 183 ·

Is it not a shame that we are always afraid of Christ, whereas there was never in heaven or earth a more loving, familiar, or milder man, in words, works, and demeanour, especially towards poor, sorrowful, and tormented consciences? Hence, the prophet Jeremiah prays, saying: "O Lord, grant that we be not afraid of thee."

· 184 ·

It is written in Psalm li.: "Behold, thou requirest truth in the inward parts, and shalt make me to understand wisdom secretly." This is that mystery which is hidden from the world, and will remain hidden; it is the truth that lies in the inward parts, and the secret wisdom; not the wisdom of the lawyers, of the physicians, philosophers, and of the crafty ones of the world; no; but thy wisdom, O Lord! which thou hast made me to understand. This is that golden art which Sadoleto had not, though he wrote much of this psalm.

· 185 ·

The preaching of the apostles went forth, and
powerfully sounded through the whole world, after
Christ's resurrection, when he had sent the Holy
Ghost. This master, the Holy Ghost, worked through
the apostles, and showed the doctrine of Christ
clearly, so that their preaching produced more fruit
than when Christ preached, as he himself before
had declared, saying: "He that believeth in me,
shall do also the works that I do, and shall do
greater than these."

Christ by force would not break through with
his preaching, as he might have done, for he
preached so powerfully that the people were astonished at his doctrine, but proceeded softly and
mildly in regard to the fathers, to whom he was
promised, and of those that much esteemed them,
to the end he might take away and abolish the
ceremonial law, together with its service and worship.

· 186 ·

Christ preached without wages, yet the godly
women, whom he had cleansed and made whole,
and delivered from wicked spirits and diseases,
ministered unto him of that which they had (Luke

viii.). They gave him supply, and he also took and received that which others freely and willingly gave him (John xix.).

When he sent the apostles forth to preach, he said: Freely ye have received, therefore freely give, &c., wherein he forbids them not to take something for their pains and work, but that they should not take care and sorrow for food and raiment, &c., for whithersoever they went, they should find some people that would not see them want.

· 187 ·

The prophecies that the Son of God should take human nature upon him, are given so obscurely, that I think the devil knew not that Christ should be conceived by the Holy Ghost, and born of the Virgin Mary.

Hence, when he tempted Christ in the wilderness, he said to him: "If thou art the Son of God?" He calls him the Son of God, not that he held him so to be by descent and nature, but according to the manner of the Scripture, which names human creatures the children of God: "Ye are all the children of the Most Highest," &c. It was not desired that these prophecies of Christ's passion, resurrection, and kingdom, should be revealed before the time of his coming, save only to his prophets and other high enlightened people; it was reserved for the coming of Christ, the right and only doctor that should open the understanding.

· 188 ·

The reason why Peter and the other apostles did not expressly call Christ the Son of God, was that they would not give occasion to the godly Jews, who as yet were weak in faith, to shun and persecute their preaching, by appearing to declare a new God, and to reject the God of their fathers. Yet they mention, with express words, the office of Christ and his works; that he is a prince of life; that he raises from the dead, justifies and forgives sins, hears prayers, enlightens and comforts hearts, &c., wherewith they clearly and sufficiently show and acknowledge that he is the true God; for no creature can perform such works but God only.

· 189 ·

The devil assaults the Christian world with highest power and subtlety, vexing true Christians through tyrants, heretics, and false brethren, and instigating the whole world against them.

On the contrary, Christ resists the devil and his

kingdom, with a few simple and contemned people, as they seem in the world, weak and foolish, and yet he gets the victory.

Now, it were a very unequal war for one poor sheep to encounter a hundred wolves, as it befell the apostles, when Christ sent them out into the world, when one after another was made away with and slain. Against wolves we should rather send out lions, or more fierce and horrible beasts. But Christ has pleasure therein, to show his highest wisdom and power in our greatest weakness and foolishness, as the world conceives, and so proceeds that all shall eat their own bane, and go to the devil, who set themselves against his servants and disciples.

For he alone, the Lord of Hosts, does wonders; he preserves his sheep in the midst of wolves, and himself so afflicts them, that we plainly see our faith consists not in the power of human wisdom, but in the power of God, for although Christ permit one of his sheep to be devoured, yet he sends ten or more others in his place.

· 190 ·

Many say that Christ having by force driven the buyers and sellers out of the temple, we also may use force against the popish bishops and enemies

of God's Word, as Munzer and other seducers. But
Christ did many things which we neither may nor
can do after him. He walked upon the water, he
fasted forty days and forty nights, he raised Lazarus from death, after he had lain four days in
the grave, &c.; such and the like we must leave
undone. Much less will Christ consent that we by
force assail the enemies of the truth; he commands
the contrary: "Love your enemies, pray for them
that vex and persecute you;" "Be merciful, as your
Father is merciful;" "Take my yoke upon you and
learn of me, for I am meek and humble in heart;"
"He that will follow me, let him deny himself, take
up his cross, and follow me."

· 191 ·

'Tis a great wonder how the name of Christ has
remained in Popedom, where, for hundreds of
years, nothing was delivered to the people but the
pope's laws and decrees, that is, doctrines and commandments of men, so that it had been no marvel
if the name of Christ and his word had been forgotten.

But God wonderfully preserved his gospel in the
church, which now from the pulpits is taught to the
people, word by word. In like manner, it is a special

great work of God, that the Creed, the Lord's Prayer, Baptism, and the Lord's Supper, have remained and cleaved to the hearts of those who were ordained to receive them in the midst of Popedom.

God has also often awakened pious learned men, who revealed his Word, and gave them courage openly to reprove the false doctrines and abuses that were crept into the church, as John Huss, and others.

· 192 ·

The kingdom of Christ is a kingdom of grace, mercy, and of all comfort; Psalm cxvii.: "His grace and truth is ever more and more towards us." The kingdom of Antichrist, the pope, is a kingdom of lies and destruction; Psalm x.: "His mouth is full of cursing, fraud, and deceit; under his tongue is ungodliness and vanity." The kingdom of Mohammed is a kingdom of revenge, of wrath, and desolation, Ezek. xxxviii.

· 193 ·

The weak in faith also belong to the kingdom of Christ; otherwise the Lord would not have said to Peter, "Strengthen thy brethren," Luke, xxii.; and Rom. xiv.: "Receive the weak in faith;" also I

Thess. v.: "Comfort the feeble-minded, support the weak." If the weak in faith did not belong to Christ, where, then, would the apostles have been, whom the Lord oftentimes, as after his resurrection, Mark, xvi., reproved because of their unbelief?

· 194 ·

A cup of water, if a man can have no better, is good to quench the thirst. A morsel of bread stills the hunger, and he that needs it seeks it earnestly. Christ is the best, surest, and only physic against the most fearful enemy of mankind, the devil; but men believe it not with their hearts. If they want a physician, living a hundred miles off, who, they think, can drive away temporal death, oh, how diligently is he sent for—no money or cost is spared! But the small and little heap only stick fast to the true physician, and by his art learn that which the holy Simeon well knew by reason of which he joyfully sang: "Lord, now lettest thou thy servant depart in peace, for mine eyes have seen thy salvation!" Whence came his great joy? Because that with spiritual and corporal eyes he saw the Saviour of the world, the true physician against sin and death. 'Tis a great pain to behold how desirous a thirsty man is of drink, or a hungry man of food, though a cup of water or morsel of bread can still hunger and thirst no longer than two or three hours, while no man, or very few, desires or longs after the most precious of all physicians, though he lovingly calls us to come unto him, saying, "He that is athirst, let him come to me and drink," John, vii.

· 195 ·

Even as Christ is now invisible and unknown to the world, so are we Christians also invisible and unknown therein. "Your life," says St. Paul, Coloss. iii., "is hid with Christ in God." Therefore the world knows us not, much less does it see Christ in us. But we and the world are easily parted; they care nothing for us, and we nothing for them; Christ the world is crucified unto us, and we to the world. Let them go with their wealth, and leave us to our minds and manners.

When we have our sweet and loving Saviour Christ, we are rich and happy more than enough; we care nothing for their state, honour, and wealth. But we often lose our Saviour Christ, and little think that he is in us, and we in him; that he is ours, and we are his. Yet although he hide from us, as we think, in the time of need, for a moment,

yet are we comforted in his promise, where he says,
"I am daily with you to the world's end;" this is
our richest treasure.

· 196 ·

Christ desires nothing more of us than that we
speak of him. But thou wilt say: If I speak or
preach of him, then the word freezes upon my lips.
O, regard not that, but hear what Christ says:
"Ask, and it shall be given unto you," &c.; and, "I
am with him in trouble," "I will deliver him, and
bring him to honour," &c. Also: "Call upon me in
the time of trouble, so will I hear thee, and thou
shalt praise me," &c., Psalm 1. How could we perform a more easy service of God, without all labour
or charge? There is no work on earth easier than
the true service of God; he loads us with no heavy
burthens, but only asks that we believe in him and
preach of him. True, thou mayest be sure thou shalt
be persecuted for this, but our sweet Saviour gives
us a comfortable promise: "I will be with you in
the time of trouble, and will help you out," &c.,
Luke, xii. 7. I make no such promise to my servant
when I set him to work, either to plough or to cart,
as Christ to me, that he will help me in my need.
We only fail in belief: if I had faith according as

the Scriptures requires of me, I alone would drive
the Turk out of Constantinople, and the pope out of
Rome; but it comes far short; I must rest satisfied
with that which Christ spake to St. Paul: "My grace
is sufficient for thee, for my power is strong in
weakness."

· 197 ·

The greatest wonder ever on earth is, that the
Son of God died the shameful death of the cross.
It is astonishing, that the Father should say to his
only Son, who by nature is God: Go, let them hang
thee on the gallows. The love of the everlasting
Father was immeasurably greater towards his only
begotten Son than the love of Abraham towards
Isaac; for the Father testifies from heaven: "This
is my beloved Son, in whom I am well pleased;"
yet he was cast away so lamentably, like a worm, a
scorn of men, and outcast of the people.

At this the blind understanding of man stumbles,
saying, Is this the only begotten Son of the everlasting Father—how, then, deals he so unmercifully
with him? he showed himself more kind to Caiaphas,
Herod, and Pilate, than towards his only beloved
Son. But to us true Christians, it is the greatest
comfort; for we therein recognise that the merciful

Lord God and Father so loved the poor condemned world, that he spared not his only begotten Son, but gave him up for us all, that whosoever believeth in him should not perish, but have everlasting life.

They who are tormented with high spiritual temptations, which every one is not able to endure, should have this example before their eyes, when they are in sorrow and heaviness of spirit, fearing God's wrath, the day of judgment, and everlasting death, and such like fiery darts of the devil. Let them comfort themselves, that although they often feel such intolerable sufferings, yet are they never the more rejected of God, but are of him better beloved, seeing he makes them like unto his only begotten Son; and let them believe, that as they suffer with him, so will he also deliver them out of their sufferings. For such as will live godly in Christ Jesus must suffer persecution; yet one more than another, according to every one's strength or weakness in faith: "For God is true, who will not suffer us to be tempted above that we are able to bear."

· 198 ·

When Jesus Christ utters a word, he opens his mouth so wide that it embraces all heaven and earth, even though that word be but in a whisper. The word of the emperor is powerful, but that of Jesus Christ governs the whole universe.

· 199 ·

I expect more goodness from Kate my wife, from Philip Melancthon, and from other friends, than from my sweet and blessed Saviour Christ Jesus; and yet I know for certain, that neither she nor any other person on earth, will or can suffer that for me which he has suffered; why then should I be afraid of him! This my foolish weakness grieves me very much. We plainly see in the gospel, how mild and gentle he showed himself towards his disciples; how kindly he passed over their weakness, their presumption, yea, their foolishness. He checked their unbelief, and in all gentleness admonished them. Moreover, the Scripture, which is most sure, says: "Well are all they that put their trust in him." Fie on our unbelieving hearts, that we should be afraid of this man, who is more loving, friendly, gentle, and compassionate towards us than are our kindred, our brethren and sisters; yea, than parents themselves are towards their own children.

He that has such temptations, let him be assured,

it is not Christ, but the envious devil that affrights,
wounds, and would destroy him; for Christ comforts, heals, and revives.

Oh! his grace and goodness towards us is so immeasurably great, that without great assaults and
trials it cannot be understood. If the tyrants and
false brethren had not set themselves so fiercely
against me, my writings and proceedings, then
should I have vaunted myself too much of my poor
gifts and qualities; nor should I with such fervency
of heart have directed my prayers to God for his
divine assistance; I should not have ascribed all to
God's grace, but to mine own dexterity and power,
and so should have flown to the devil. But to the
end this might be prevented, my gracious Lord and
Saviour Christ caused me to be chastised; he ordained that the devil should plague and torment me
with his fiery darts, inwardly and outwardly,
through tyrants, as the pope and other heretics, and
all this he suffered to be done for my good. "It is
good for me that I have been in trouble, that I may
learn thy statutes."

· 200 ·

I know nothing of Jesus Christ but only his
name; I have not heard or seen him corporally, yet

I have, God be praised, learned so much out of the Scriptures, that I am well and thoroughly satisfied; therefore I desire neither to see nor to hear him in the body. When left and forsaken of all men, in my highest weakness, in trembling, and in fear of death, when persecuted of the wicked world, then I felt most deeply the divine power which this name, Christ Jesus, communicated unto me.

· 201 ·

It is no wonder that Satan is an enemy to Christ, his people and kingdom, and sets himself against him and his word, with all his power and cunning. 'Tis an old hate and grudge between them, which began in Paradise; for they are, by nature and kind, of contrary minds and dispositions. The devil smells Christ many hundred miles off; he hears at Constantinople and at Rome, what we at Wittenberg teach and preach against his kingdom; he feels also what hurt and damage he sustains thereby; therefore rages and swells he so horribly.

But what is more to be wondered at is, that we, who are of one kind and nature, and, through the bond of love, knit so fast together that each ought to love the other as himself, should have, at times, such envy, hate, wrath, discord and revenge, that one is ready to kill the other. For who is nearer allied to a man than his wife; to the son, than his father; to the daughter, than her mother; to the brother, than his sister, &c.? yet, it is most commonly found, that discord and strife are among them.

· 202 ·

It is impossible that the gospel and the law should dwell together in one heart, for of necessity either Christ must yield and give place to the law, or the law to Christ. St. Paul says: "They which will be justified through the law, are fallen from grace." Therefore, when thou art of this mind, that Christ and the confidence of the law may dwell together in thy heart, then thou mayst know for certain that it is not Christ, but the devil that dwells in thee, who under the mask and form of Christ terrifies thee. He will have, that thou make thyself righteous through the law, and through thy own good works; for the true Christ calls thee not to an account for thy sins, nor commands thee to trust in thy good works, but says: "Come unto me all ye that be weary and heavy laden, and I will give you rest," &c.

· 203 ·

I have set Christ and the pope together by the
ears, so trouble myself no further; though I get
between the door and the hinges and be squeezed,
it is no matter; Christ will go through with it.

· 204 ·

Christ once appeared visible here on earth, and
showed his glory, and according to the divine purpose of God finished the work of redemption and
the deliverance of mankind. I do not desire he
should come once more in the same manner, neither
would I he should send an angel unto me. Nay,
though an angel should come and appear before
mine eyes from heaven, yet it would not add to my
belief; for I have of my Saviour Christ Jesus bond
and seal; I have his Word, Spirit, and sacrament;
thereon I depend, and desire no new revelations.
And the more steadfastly to confirm me in this
resolution, to hold solely by God's Word, and not
to give credit to any visions or revelations, I shall
relate the following circumstance:—On Good Friday last, I being in my chamber in fervent prayer,
contemplating with myself, how Christ my Saviour
on the cross suffered and died for our sins, there

suddenly appeared upon the wall a bright vision
of our Saviour Christ, with the five wounds, steadfastly looking upon me, as if it had been Christ
himself corporally. At first sight, I thought it had
been some celestial revelation, but I reflected that
it must needs be an illusion and juggling of the
devil, for Christ appeared to us in his Word, and in
a meaner and more humble form; therefore I spake
to the vision thus: Avoid thee, confounded devil:
I know no other Christ than he who was crucified,
and who in his Word is pictured and presented
unto me. Whereupon the image vanished, clearly
showing of whom it came.

· 205 ·

Alas! what is our wit and wisdom? before we
understand anything as we ought, we lie down and
die, so that the devil has a good chance with us.
When one is thirty years old, he has still *Stultitias
carnales*; yea also, *Stultitias spirituales*; and yet 'tis
much to be admired at, how in such our imbecility
and weakness, we achieve and accomplish much
and great matters, but 'tis God does it. God gave to
Alexander the Great wisdom and good success; yet
he calls him, in the prophet Jeremiah, a youth,
where he says, a young boy shall perform it; he

shall come and turn the city Tyre upside down.
Yet Alexander could not leave off his foolishness,
for often he swilled himself drunk, and in his
drunkenness stabbed his best and worthiest friends,
and afterwards drank himself to death at Babylon.
Solomon was not above twenty when he was made
king, but he was well instructed by Nathan, and
desired wisdom, which was pleasing to God, as the
text says: But now, chests full of money are desired.
O! say we now, if I had but money, then I would
do so and so.

· 206 ·

Christ said to the heathen woman: I am not sent
but to the lost sheep of the house of Israel; yet
afterwards he helped both her and her daughter;
therefore a man might say: Christ here contradicted
himself. I reply: True, Christ was not sent to the
Gentiles, but when the Gentiles came unto him, he
would not reject or put them from him. In person
he was sent only to the Jews, and therefore he
preached in the land of the Jews. But through the
apostles his doctrine went into the whole world.
And St. Paul names the Lord Christ, *ministrum
circumcisionis*, by reason of the promise which God
gave to the fathers. The Jews themselves boast of

God's justness in performing what he promised, but
we Gentiles boast of God's mercy; God has not
forgotten us Gentiles. Indeed, God spake not with
us, neither had we king or prophet with whom God
spake; but St. Paul, in another place, says: It was
necessary that the word should first be preached
to you, but seeing you will not receive it, lo! we
turn to the Gentiles. At this the Jews are much
offended to this day; they flatter themselves: Messiah is only and alone for them and theirs. Indeed,
it is a glorious name and title that Moses gives
them: Thou art an holy nation: but David, in his
psalm, afterwards promises Christ to the Gentiles:
"Praise the Lord all ye nations."

· 207 ·

We should consider the histories of Christ three
manner of ways; first, as a history of acts or
legends; secondly, as a gift or a present; thirdly, as
an example, which we should believe and follow.

· 208 ·

Christ, our blessed Saviour, forbore to preach
and teach until the thirtieth year of his age, neither
would he openly be heard; no, though he beheld
and heard so many impieties, abominable idolatries.

heresies, blasphemings of God, &c. It was a wonderful thing he could abstain, and with patience endure them, until the time came that he was to appear in his office of preaching.

OF THE HOLY GHOST

· 209 ·

THE Holy Ghost has two offices: first, He is a Spirit of grace, that makes God gracious unto us, and receive us as his acceptable children, for Christ's sake. Secondly, He is a Spirit of prayer, that prays for us, and for the whole world, to the end that all evil may be turned from us, and that all good may happen to us. The spirit of grace teaches people; the spirit of prayer prays. It is a wonder how one thing is accomplished various ways. It is one thing to have the Holy Spirit as a spirit of prophecy, and another to have the revealing of the same; for many have had the Holy Spirit before the birth of Christ, and yet he was not revealed unto them.

We do not separate the Holy Ghost from faith; neither do we teach that he is against faith; for he is the certainty itself in the world, that makes us sure and certain of the Word; so that, without all wavering or doubting, we certainly believe that it is even so and no otherwise than as God's Word says and is delivered unto us. But the Holy Ghost is given to none without the Word.

Mohammad, the pope, papists, Antinomians, and other sectaries, have no certainty at all, neither can they be sure of these things; for they depend not on God's Word, but on their own righteousness. And when they have done many and great works, yet they always stand in doubt, and say: Who knows whether this which we have done be pleasing to God or no; or, whether we have done works enough or no? They must continually think with themselves, We are still unworthy.

But a true and godly Christian, between these two doubts, is sure and certain, and says: I nothing regard these doubtings; I neither look upon my holiness, nor upon my unworthiness, but I believe in Jesus Christ, who is both holy and worthy; and whether I be holy or unholy, yet I am sure and certain, that Christ gives himself, with all his holiness, worthiness, and what he is and has, to be mine own. For my part, I am a poor sinner, and that I am sure of out of God's Word. Therefore, the Holy Ghost only and alone is able to say: Jesus Christ is the Lord; the Holy Ghost teaches, preaches, and declares Christ.

The Holy Ghost goes first and before in what pertains to teaching; but in what concerns hearing, the Word goes first and before, and then the Holy Ghost follows after. For we must first hear the Word, and then afterwards the Holy Ghost works in our hearts; he works in the hearts of whom he will, and how he will, but never without the Word.

· 210 ·

The Holy Ghost began his office and work openly on Whitsunday; for he gave to the apostles and disciples of Christ a true and certain comfort in their hearts, and a secure and joyful courage, insomuch that they regarded not whether the world and the devil were merry or sad, friends or enemies, angry or pleased. They went in all security up and down the streets of the city, and doubtless they had these, or the like thoughts: We regard neither Annas nor Caiaphas, Pilate nor Herod; they are nothing worth, we all in all; they are our subjects and servants, we their lords and rulers.

So went the loving apostles on, in all courage, without seeking leave or licence.

They asked not whether they should preach or no, or whether the priests and people would allow it. O, no! They went on boldly, they opened their mouths freely, and reproved all the people, rulers and subjects, as murderers, wicked wretches, and traitors, who had slain the Prince of Life.

And this spirit, so needful and necessary at that time for the apostles and disciples, is now needful for us; for our adversaries accuse us, like as were the apostles, as rebels and disturbers of the peace of the Church. Whatsoever evil happens, that, say they, have we done or caused. In Popedom, say they, it was not so evil as it is since this doctrine came in; now we have all manner of mischiefs, dearth, wars, and the Turks. Of this they lay all the fault to our preaching, and, if they could, would charge us with being the cause of the devil's falling from heaven; yea, would say we had crucified and slain Christ also.

Therefore the Whitsuntide sermons of the Holy Ghost are very needful for us, that thereby we may be comforted, and with boldness contemn and slight such blaspheming, and that the Holy Ghost may put boldness and courage into our hearts, that we may stoutly thrust ourselves forward, let who will be offended, and let who will reproach us, and, that although sects and heresies arise, we may not regard them. Such a courage there must be that cares for nothing, but boldly and freely acknowledges and preaches Christ, who of wicked hands was crucified and slain.

The preached gospel is offensive in all places of the world, rejected and condemned.

If the gospel did not offend and anger citizen or countryman, prince or bishop, then it would be a fine and an acceptable preaching, and might well be tolerated, and people would willingly hear and receive it. But seeing it is a kind of preaching which makes people angry, especially the great and powerful, and deep-learned ones of the world, great courage is necessary, and the Holy Ghost, to those that intend to preach it.

It was, indeed, undaunted courage in the poor fishers, the apostles, to stand up and preach so that the whole council at Jerusalem were offended, to bring upon themselves the wrath of the whole government, spiritual and temporal—yea, of the Roman emperor himself. Truly, this could not have been done without the Holy Ghost. 'Twas a great wonder that the high-priest, and Pontius Pilate, did not cause these preachers that hour to be put to death, what they said smacking so much of rebellion against the spiritual and temporal government; yet both high-priest and Pilate were struck with fear, to the end that God might show his power in the apostles' weakness.

Thus it is with the church of Christ: it goes on in apparent weakness; and yet in its weakness, there is such mighty strength and power, that all the worldly wise and powerful must stand amazed thereat and fear.

· 211 ·

It is testified by Holy Scripture, and the Nicæan creed out of Holy Scripture teaches that the Holy Ghost is he who makes alive, and, together with the Father and the Son, is worshipped and glorified.

Therefore the Holy Ghost, of necessity, must be true and everlasting God with the Father and the Son, in one only essence. For if he were not true and everlasting God, then could not be attributed and given unto him the divine power and honour that he makes alive, and together with the Father and the Son is worshipped and glorified; on this point the Fathers powerfully set themselves against the heretics, upon the strength of Holy Scripture.

The Holy Ghost is not such a comforter as the world is, where neither truth nor constancy is, but he is a true, an everlasting, and a constant comforter, without deceit and lies; he is one whom no man can deceive. He is called a witness, because he bears witness only of Christ and of none other; without his testimony concerning Christ, there is no true or firm comfort. Therefore all rests on this, that we take sure hold of the text, and say: I believe in Jesus Christ, who died for me; and I know that the Holy Ghost, who is called, and is a witness and a comforter, preaches and witnesses in Christendom of none, but only of Christ, therewith to strengthen and comfort all sad and sorrowful hearts. Thereon will I also remain, depending upon none other for comfort. Our blessed Saviour Christ himself preaches that the Holy Ghost is everlasting and Almighty God. Otherwise he would not have directed his commission thus: Go, and teach all nations, and baptize them in the name of the Father, of the Son, and of the Holy Ghost, and teach them to keep and observe all things whatsoever I have commanded of you. It must needs follow, that the Holy Ghost is true, eternal God, equal in power and might with the Father and the Son, without all end. Likewise Christ says: "And I will pray the

Father, and he shall give you another comforter,
that he may abide with you for ever; even the
Spirit of Truth, whom the world cannot receive,
because it seeth him not, neither knoweth him."
Mark well this sentence, for herein we find the difference of the three persons distinctly held out unto
us: "I will pray the Father, and he shall give you
another comforter." Here we have two persons—
Christ the Son that prays, and the Father that is
prayed unto. Now, if the Father shall give such a
comforter, then the Father himself cannot be that
comforter; neither can Christ, that prays, be the
same; so that very significantly the three persons
are here plainly pictured and portrayed unto us.
For even as the Father and the Son are two distinct
and sundry persons, so the third person of the Holy
Ghost is another distinct person, and yet notwithstanding there is but one only everlasting God.

Now, what the same third person is, Christ
teaches (John, xv.) : "But when the Comforter is
come, whom I will send unto you from the Father,
even the Spirit of Truth, which proceedeth from the
Father, he shall testify of me."

In this place, Christ speaks not only of the office
and work of the Holy Ghost, but also of his essence and substance, and says: "He proceedeth from

the Father;" that is, his proceeding is without beginning, and is everlasting. Therefore the holy prophets attribute and give unto him this title, and call him "The Spirit of the Lord."

OF SINS

· 212 ·

NONE of the Fathers of the Church made mention of original sin until Augustin came, who made a difference between original and actual sin; namely, that original sin is to covet, lust, and desire, which is the root and cause of actual sin; such lust and desire in the faithful, God forgives, imputing it not unto them, for the sake of Christ, seeing they resist it by the assistance of the Holy Ghost. As St. Paul, Rom. viii. The papists and other sinners oppose the known truth. St. Paul says: "A man that is an heretic after the first and second admonition, rejects," knowing that such an one sins, being condemned of himself. And Christ says: "Let them alone, they are blind leaders of the blind." If one

err through ignorance, he will be instructed; but if
he be hardened, and will not yield to the truth, like
Pharaoh, who would not acknowledge his sins, or
humble himself before God, and therefore was destroyed in the Red Sea, even so will he be destroyed.
We are all sinners by nature—conceived and born
in sin; sin has poisoned us through and through;
we have from Adam a will, which continually sets
itself against God, unless by the Holy Ghost it be
renewed and changed. Of this neither the philosophers nor the lawyers know anything; therefore
they are justly excluded from the circuit of divinity,
not grounding their doctrine upon God's word.

· 213 ·

Sins against the Holy Ghost are, first, presumption; second, despair; third, opposition to and
condemnation of the known truth; fourth, not to
wish well, but to grudge one's brother or neighbour the grace of God; fifth, to be hardened; sixth,
to be impenitent.

· 214 ·

We have within us many sins against our Lord
God, and which justly displease him: such as anger,

impatience, covetousness, greediness, incontinence,
hatred, malice, &c. These are great sins, which
everywhere in the world go on with power, and get
the upper hand. Yet these are nothing in comparison of contemning of God's word; yea, all these
would remain uncommitted, if we did but love and
reverence that. But, alas! the whole world is
drowned in this sin. No man cares a fillip for the
gospel, all snarl at and persecute it, holding it as
no sin. I behold with wonder in the church, that
among the hearers, one looks this way, another
that; and that among so great a multitude, few
come to hear the sermon. This sin is so common,
that people will not confess it to be like other sins;
every one deems it a slight thing to hear a discourse
without attention, and not diligently to mark, learn,
and inwardly digest it. It is not so about other sins;
as murder, adultery, thieving, &c. For, after these
sins, in due time follow grief, sorrow of heart, and
remorse. But not to hear God's word with diligence,
yea, to contemn, to persecute it, of this man makes
no account. Yet it is a sin so fearful, that for the
committing it both land and people must be destroyed, as it went with Jerusalem, with Rome,
Greece, and other kingdoms.

· 215 ·

Christ well knew how to discriminate sins; we see in the gospel how harsh he was towards the Pharisees, by reason of their great hatred and envy against him and his Word, while, on the contrary, how mild and friendly he was towards the woman who was a sinner. That same envy will needs rob Christ of his word, for he is a bitter enemy unto it, and in the end will crucify it. But the woman, as the greatest sinner, takes hold on the Word, hears Christ, and believes that he is the only Saviour of the world; she washes his feet, and anoints him with a costly water.

· 216 ·

Let us not think ourselves more just than was the poor sinner and murderer on the cross. I believe if the apostles had not fallen, they would not have believed in the remission of sins. Therefore, when the devil upbraids me, touching my sins, then I say: Good St. Peter, although I am a great sinner, yet I have not denied Christ my Saviour, as you did. In such instances the forgiveness of sins remains confirmed. And although the apostles were sinners, yet our Saviour Christ always excused them, as when they plucked the ears of corn; but, on the con-

trary, he jeered the Pharisees touching the paying
of tribute, and commonly showed his disapproba-
tion of them; but the disciples he always comforted,
as Peter, where he says: "Fear not, thou shalt hence-
forth catch men."

· 217 ·

No sinner can escape his punishment, unless he
be sorry for his sins. For though one go scot-free for
awhile, yet at last he will be snapped, as the Psalm
says: "God indeed is still judge on earth."

Our Lord God suffers the ungodly to be surprised
and taken captive in very slight and small things,
when they think not of it, when they are most secure, and live in delight and pleasure, leaping for
joy. In such manner was the Pope surprised by me,
about his indulgences and pardons, comparatively a
slight matter.

· 218 ·

A magistrate, a father or mother, a master or
dame, tradesmen and others, must now and then
look through the fingers at their citizens, children,
and servants, if their faults and offences be not too
gross and frequent; for where we will have *sum-
mum jus*, there follows often *summa injuria*, so

that all must go to wreck. Neither do they which
are in office always hit it aright, but err and sin
themselves, and must therefore desire the forgiveness of sins.

God forgives sins merely out of grace for Christ's
sake; but we must not abuse the grace of God. God
has given signs and tokens enough, that our sins
shall be forgiven; namely, the preaching of the
gospel, baptism, the Lord's Supper, and the Holy
Ghost in our hearts.

Now it is also needful we testify in our works
that we have received the forgiveness of sins, by
each forgiving the faults of his brother. There is
no comparison between God's remitting of sins and
ours. For what are one hundred pence, in comparison of ten thousand pounds? as Christ says, nought.
And although we deserve nothing by our forgiving,
yet we must forgive, that thereby we may prove
and give testimony that we from God have received
forgiveness of our sins.

The forgiveness of sins is declared only in God's
Word, and there we must seek it; for it is grounded
on God's promises. God forgives thee thy sins, not
because thou feelest them and art sorry, for this
sin itself produces, without deserving, but he for-

gives thy sins because he is merciful, and because he has promised to forgive for Christ's sake.

· 219 ·

When God said to Cain, through Adam: "If thou do well, shalt thou not be accepted? And if thou dost not well, sin lieth at the door," he shows the appearance of sinners, and speaks with Cain as with the most hypocritical and poisonous Capuchin: 'twas as if Adam had said: Thou hast heard how it went with me in Paradise; I also would willingly have hid my offence with fig leaves, lurking behind a tree, but know, good fellow, our Lord God will not be so deceived; the fig leaves would not serve the turn.

Ah! it was, doubtless, to Adam, a heart-breaking and painful task, when he was compelled to banish and proscribe his first-born and only son, to hunt him out of his house, and to say: Depart from me, and come no more in my sight; I still feel what I have already lost in Paradise, I will lose no more for thy sake; I will now, with more diligence, take heed to my God's commands. And no doubt Adam afterwards preached with redoubled diligence.

· 220 ·

These two sins, hatred and pride, deck and trim
themselves out, as the devil clothed himself, in the
Godhead. Hatred will be godlike; pride will be
truth. These two are right deadly sins: hatred is
killing; pride is lying.

· 221 ·

It can be hurtful to none to acknowledge and confess his sins. Hast thou done this or that sin?—what
then? We freely, in God's name, acknowledge the
same, and deny it not, but from our hearts say: O
Lord God! I have done this sin.

Although thou hast not committed this or that
sin, yet, nevertheless, thou art an ungodly creature;
and if thou hast not done that sin which another has
done, so has he not committed that sin which thou
hast done; therefore cry quits one with another.
'Tis as the man said, that had young wolves to sell;
he was asked which of them was the best? He answered: If one be good, then they are all good; they
are all like one another. If thou hast been a murderer, an adulterer, a drunkard, &c., so have I been
a blasphemer of God, who for the space of fifteen
years was a friar, and blasphemed God with cele-
brating that abominable idol, the mass. It had been

better for me I had been a partaker of other great wickednesses instead; but what is done cannot be undone; he that has stolen, let him henceforward steal no more.

· 222 ·

The sins of common, untutored people are nothing in comparison with the sins committed by great and high persons, that are in spiritual and temporal offices.

What are the sins done by a poor wretch, that according to law and justice is hanged, or the offences of a poor strumpet, compared with the sins of a false teacher, who daily makes away with many poor people, and kills them both body and soul? The sins committed against the first table of God's ten commandments, are not so much regarded by the world, as those committed against the second table.

· 223 ·

Original sin, after regeneration, is like a wound that begins to heal; though it be a wound, yet it is in course of healing, though it still runs and is sore.

So original sin remains in Christians until they die, yet itself is mortified and continually dying.

Its head is crushed in pieces, so that it cannot condemn us.

· 224 ·

All natural inclinations are either without God or against him; therefore none are good. I prove it thus: All affections, desires, and inclinations of mankind are evil, wicked, and spoiled, as the Scripture says.

Experience testifies this: for no man is so virtuous as to marry a wife, only thereby to have children, to love and to bring them up in the fear of God.

No hero undertakes great enterprises for the common good, but out of ambition, for which he is justly condemned: hence it must needs follow, that such original, natural desires and inclinations are wicked. But God bears with them and lets them pass, in those that believe in Christ.

· 225 ·

Schenck proceeds in a most monstrous manner, haranguing, without the least discernment, on the subject of sin. I, myself, have heard him say, in the pulpit at Eisenach, without any qualification whatever, "Sin, sin is nothing; God will receive sinners;

He himself tells us they shall enter the kingdom of heaven." Schenck makes no distinction between sins committed, sins committing, and sins to be committed, so that when the common people hear him say, "Sin, for God will receive sinners;" they very readily repeat, "Well, we'll sin then." 'Tis a most erroneous doctrine. What is announced as to God's receiving sinners, applies to sinners who have repented; there is all the difference in the world between *agnitum peccatum*, attended by repentance, and *velle peccare* which is an inspiration of the devil.

OF FREE-WILL

· 226 ·

THE very name, Free-will, was odious to all the Fathers. I, for my part, admit that God gave to mankind a free-will, but the question is, whether this same freedom be in our power and strength, or no? We may very fitly call it a subverted, perverse, fickle, and wavering will, for it is only God that works in us, and we must suffer and be subject to his pleasure. Even as a potter out of his clay makes a pot or vessel, as he wills, so it is for our free-will, to suffer and not to work. It stands not in our strength; for we are not able to do anything that is good in divine matters.

· 227 ·

I have often been resolved to live uprightly, and to lead a true godly life, and to set everything aside that would hinder this, but it was far from being put in execution; even as it was with Peter, when he swore he would lay down his life for Christ.

I will not lie or dissemble before my God, but will freely confess, I am not able to effect that good which I intend, but await the happy hour when God shall be pleased to meet me with his grace.

The will of mankind is either presumptuous or despairing. No human creature can satisfy the law. For the law of God discourses with me, as it were after this manner: Here is a great, a high, and a steep mountain, and thou must go over it; whereupon my flesh and free-will say, I will go over it; but my conscience says, Thou canst not go over it; then comes despair, and says, If I cannot, then I must forbear. In this sort does the law work in mankind either presumption or despair; yet the

law must be preached and taught, for if we preach
not the law, then people grow rude and confident,
whereas if we preach it, we make them afraid.

· 228 ·

Saint Augustin writes, that free-will, without
God's grace and the Holy Ghost, can do nothing but
sin; which sentence sorely troubles the school-
divines. They say, Augustin spoke *hyperbolicè,* and
too much; for they understand that part of Scripture to be spoken only of those people who lived
before the deluge, which says: "And God saw that
the wickedness of man was great in the earth, and
that every imagination of the thoughts of his heart
was only evil continually," &c.; whereas He speaks
in a general way, which these poor school-divines
do not see any more than what the Holy Ghost says,
soon after the deluge, in almost the same words:
"And the Lord said in his heart, I will not again
curse the ground any more for man's sake, for the
imagination of man's heart is evil from his youth."

Hence, we conclude in general, that man, without the Holy Ghost and God's grace, can do nothing
but sin; he proceeds therein without intermission,
and from one sin falls into another. Now, if man
will not suffer wholesome doctrine, but contemns

the all-saving Word, and resists the Holy Ghost, then through the effects and strength of his free-will he becomes God's enemy; he blasphemes the Holy Ghost, and follows the lusts and desires of his own heart, as examples in all times clearly show.

But we must diligently weigh the words which the Holy Ghost speaks through Moses: "Every imagination of the thoughts of his heart is evil continually:" so that what a man is able to conceive with his thoughts, with his understanding and free-will, by highest diligence, is evil, and not once or twice, but evil continually; without the Holy Ghost, man's reason, will, and understanding, are without the knowledge of God; and to be without the knowledge of God, is nothing else than to be ungodly, to walk in darkness, and to hold that for best which is direct worst.

I speak only of that which is good in divine things, and according to the holy Scripture; for we must make a difference between that which is temporal, and that which is spiritual, between politics and divinity; for God also allows of the government of the ungodly, and rewards their virtues, yet only so far as belongs to this temporal life; for man's will and understanding conceive that to be good which is external and temporal— nay, take it to be, not only good, but the chief good.

But when we divines speak of free-will, we ask what man's free-will is able to accomplish in divine and spiritual matters, not in outward and temporal affairs: and we conclude that man, without the Holy Ghost, is altogether wicked before God, although he were decked up and trimmed with all the virtues of the heathen, and had all their works.

For, indeed, there are fair and glorious examples in heathendom, of many virtues, where men were temperate, chaste, bountiful: loved their country, parents, wives, and children; were men of courage, and behaved themselves magnanimously and generously.

But the ideas of mankind concerning God, the true worship of God, and God's will, are altogether stark blindness and darkness. For the light of human wisdom, reason, and understanding, which alone is given to man, comprehends only what is good and profitable outwardly. And although we see that the heathen philosophers now and then discoursed touching God and his wisdom very pertinently, so that some have made prophets of Socrates, of Xenophon, of Plato, &c., yet, because they knew not that God sent his son Christ to save sinners, such

fair, glorious, and wise-seeming speeches and disputations are nothing but mere blindness and ignorance.

· 229 ·

Ah, Lord God! why should we boast of our free-
will, as if it were able to do anything ever so small,
in divine and spiritual matters? when we consider
what horrible miseries the devil has brought upon
us through sin, we might shame ourselves to death.

For, first, free-will led us into original sin, and
brought death upon us: afterwards, upon sin followed not only death, but all manner of mischiefs,
as we daily find in the world, murder, lying, de-
ceiving, stealing, and other evils, so that no man is
safe the twinkling of an eye, in body or goods, but
always stands in danger.

And, besides these evils, is afflicted with yet a
greater, as is noted in the gospel—namely, that he
is possessed of the devil, who makes him mad and
raging.

We know not rightly what we became after the
fall of our first parents; what from our mothers we
have brought with us. For we have altogether a confounded, corrupt, and poisoned nature, both in

body and soul; throughout the whole of man is nothing that is good.

This is my absolute opinion: he that will maintain that man's free-will is able to do or work anything in spiritual cases, be they never so small, denies Christ. This I have always maintained in my writings, especially in those against Erasmus, one of the learnedest men in the whole world, and thereby will I remain, for I know it to be the truth, though all the world should be against it; yea, the decree of Divine Majesty must stand fast against the gates of hell.

I confess that mankind has a free-will, but it is to milk kine, to build houses, &c., and no further; for so long as a man is at ease and in safety, and is in no want, so long he thinks he has a free-will, which is able to do something; but when want and need appear, so that there is neither meat, drink, nor money, where is then free-will? It is utterly lost, and cannot stand when it comes to the pinch. Faith only stands fast and sure, and seeks Christ. Therefore faith is far another thing than free-will; nay, free-will is nothing at all, but faith is all in all. Art thou bold and stout, and canst thou carry it lustily with thy free-will when plague, wars, and times of dearth and famine are at hand? No: in time of plague, thou knowest not what to do for fear; thou wishest thyself a hundred miles off. In time of dearth thou thinkest: Where shall I find to eat? Thy will cannot so much as give thy heart the smallest comfort in these times of need, but the longer thou strivest, the more it makes thy heart faint and feeble, insomuch that it is affrighted even at the rushing and shaking of a leaf. These are the valiant acts our free-will can achieve.

OF THE LAW AND THE GOSPEL

· 230 ·

WE must reject those who so highly boast of Moses's laws, as to temporal affairs, for we have our written imperial and country laws, under which we live, and unto which we are sworn. Neither Naaman the Assyrian, nor Job, nor Joseph, nor Daniel, nor many other good and godly Jews, observed Moses's laws out of their country, but those of the Gentiles among whom they lived.

Moses's laws bound and obliged only the Jews in that place which God made choice of. Now they are free. If we should keep and observe the laws and rites of Moses, we must also be circumcised, and keep the Mosaical ceremonies; for there is no difference; he that holds one to be necessary, must hold the rest so too. Therefore let us leave Moses to his laws, excepting only the *Moralia*, which God has planted in nature, as the Ten Commandments, which concern God's true worshipping and service, and a civil life.

· 231 ·

The particular and only office of the law is, as St. Paul teaches, that transgressions thereby should be acknowledged; for it was added, because of transgressions, till the seed should come, to whom the promise was made. These are the express and plain words of St. Paul; therefore we trouble not ourselves with what the papists allege to the contrary, and spin out of human reason, extolling the maintainers and seeming observers of Moses's law.

· 232 ·

God gives to the emperor the sword, the emperor delivers it to the judge, and causes thieves, murderers, &c., to be punished and executed. Afterwards, when God pleases, he takes the sword from the emperor again; even so does God touching the law; he leaves it to the devil, and permits him therewith to affright sinners.

· 233 ·

Never was a bolder, harsher sermon preached in the world than that wherein St. Paul abolished Moses and his law, as insufficient for a sinner's salvation.

Hence the continual dissension and strife which this apostle had with the Jews. And if Moses had not cashiered and put himself out of his office, with these words: "The Lord thy God will raise up unto thee another prophet out of thy brethren, him shalt thou hear;" who then would or could have believed the gospel, and forsaken Moses?

Hence the vehement accusation brought by the worthy Jews, who suborned certain men to accuse the beloved Stephen, saying: "We have heard him speak blasphemous words against Moses and against God." Likewise, "This man ceaseth not to speak blasphemous words against the holy place and the law," &c. For to preach and teach that the observing of the law was not necessary to salvation, was to the Jews as horrible, as though one should stand up and preach among us Christians: Christ is not the Lamb of God, that taketh away the sins of the world. St. Paul could have been content they had kept and observed the law, had they not asserted it was necessary to salvation. But the Jews would no more endure this, than the papists, with their fopperies, will now endure that we hold and observe the ceremonies, so that every one shall be at liberty either to observe or not observe them, according as occasion serves, and that the conscience therein may not be bound or ensnared, and that God's Word freely be preached and taught. But Jews and papists are ungodly wretches; they are two stockings made of one piece of cloth.

· 234 ·

Moses with his law is most terrible; there never was any equal to him in perplexing, affrighting, tyrannizing, threatening, preaching, and thundering; for he lays sharp hold on the conscience, and fearfully works it, but all by God's express command. When we are affrighted, feeling our sins,

God's wrath and judgments, most certainly, in the law is no justification; therein is nothing celestial and divine, but 'tis altogether of the world, which world is the kingdom of the devil. Therefore it is clear and apparent that the law can do nothing that is vivifying, saving, celestial, or divine; what it does is altogether temporal; that is, it gives us to know what evil is in the world, outwardly and inwardly. But, besides this, the Holy Ghost must come over the law, and speak thus in thy heart: God will not have thee affright thyself to death, only that through the law thou shouldest know thy misery, and yet not despair, but believe in Christ, who is the end of the law for righteousness.

· 235 ·

St. Paul now and then speaks scornfully of the law, but he means not that we should contemn the law; he would rather we should esteem and hold it precious. But where he teaches how we become justified before God, it was necessary for him so to speak; for it is far another thing when we talk how we may be justified before God, than when we talk about the law. When we have in hand the righteousness that justifies before God, we cannot too much disdain or undervalue the law.

The conscience must have regard to nothing but Christ; wherefore we must, with all diligence, endeavour to remove Moses with his law far from us out of sight, when we intend to stand justified before God.

· 236 ·

It is impossible for thy human strength, whosoever thou art, without God's assistance, when Moses sets upon thee with his law, accuses and threatens thee with God's wrath and death, to possess such peace as if no law or sin had ever been.

When thou feelest the terror of the law, thou mayest say thus: Madam Law! I have no time to hear you speak; your language is very rough and unfriendly; I would have you know that your reign is over, therefore I am now free, I will endure your bondage no longer. When we thus address the law, we shall find the difference between the law of grace and the law of thundering Moses; and how great a divine and celestial gift it is to hope against hope, when there seems nothing to hope for; and how true the speech of St. Paul is, where he says: "Through faith in Christ we are justified, and not through the works of the law." When, indeed, justification is not the matter in hand, we ought highly to esteem the law, extol it, and with St. Paul, call it good, true, spiritual, and divine, as in truth it is.

God will keep his Word through the writing-pen upon earth; the divines are the heads or quills of the pens, the lawyers the stumps. If the world will not keep the heads and quills, that is, if they will not hear the divines, they must keep the stumps, that is, they must hear the lawyers, who will teach them manners.

· 237 ·

I will have none of Moses with his law, for he is an enemy to my Lord and Saviour Christ. If Moses will go to law with me, I will give him his despatch, and say: Here stands Christ.

At the day of judgment Moses will doubtless look upon me, and say: Thou didst understand me rightly, and didst well distinguish between me and the law of faith; therefore we are now friends.

We must reject the law when it seeks to affright the conscience, and when we feel God's anger against our sins, then we must eat, drink, sleep, and be cheerful, to spite the devil. But human wisdom is more inclined to understand the law of Moses, than the law of the gospel. Old Adam will not out.

Together with the law, Satan torments the conscience by picturing Christ before our eyes, as an angry and stern judge, saying: God is an enemy to sinners, for he is a just God; thou art a sinner, therefore God is thy enemy. Hereat is the conscience dejected, beaten down, and taken captive. Now he that can make a true difference in this case, will say: Devil! thou art deceived, it is not so as thou pretendest; for God is not an enemy to all sinners, but only to the ungodly and impenitent sinners and persecutors of his word. For even as sin is two-fold, even so is righteousness two-fold also.

· 238 ·

Every law or commandment contains two profitable points; first, a promise; second, a threatening; for every law is, or should be, good, upright, and holy, Rom. vii. It commands that which is good, and forbids that which is evil: it rewards and defends the good and godly, but punishes and resists the wicked; as St. Paul says: "Rulers are not a terror to good works, but to the evil. Wilt thou then not be afraid of the power? do that which is good." And St. Peter: "For the punishment of evil-doers, and for the praise of them that do well." And the imperial laws teach the same. Now, seeing there are promises and threatenings in temporal laws, how

much more so are they fitting in God's laws, which
require upright faith. The emperor's laws, indeed,
require faith, true or feigned; for those who do
not fear or believe that the emperor will punish or
protect, observe not his laws, as we see, but those
observe them that fear and believe, whether from
the heart or not. Now, where in Scripture there is
a promise without the law, there faith only is necessary: as, when Abraham was promised that his seed
should multiply as the stars of heaven; he was not
commanded at that time to accomplish any work,
but he heard of a work which God would accomplish, and which he himself was not able to do. Thus
is Christ promised unto us, and is described to have
done a work which we cannot do; therefore in this
case, faith is needful for us, because by works we
cannot take hold thereof.

· 239 ·

If we diligently mark the world, we shall find that
it is governed merely by its conceited opinions;
sophistry, hypocrisy, and tyranny rule it; the upright, pure, and clear divine word must be their
handmaid, and by them controlled. Therefore let us
beware of sophistry, which consists not only in a
double tongue, in twisting words, which may be

construed any way, but also blossoms and flourishes in all arts and vocations, and will likewise have room and place in religion, where it has usurped a fine, fictitious colour.

Nothing is more pernicious than sophistry; we are by nature prone to believe lies rather than truth. Few people know what an evil sophistry is; Plato, the heathen writer, made thereof a wonderful definition. For my part, I compare it with a lie, which, like a snow-ball, the more it is rolled, the greater it becomes.

Therefore, I approve not of such as pervert everything, undervaluing and finding fault with other men's opinions, though they be good and sound. I like not brains that can dispute on both sides, and yet conclude nothing certain. Such sophistications are mere crafty and subtle inventions and contrivances, to cozen and deceive people.

But I love an honest and well-affected mind, that seeks after truth simply and plainly, and goes not about with fantasies and cheating tricks.

· 240 ·

St. Paul says: "What the law could not do, in that it was weak through the flesh, God sending his own Son in the likeness of sinful flesh, and for sin con-

demned sin in flesh: that the righteousness of the
law might be fulfilled in us," &c. That is, Christ is
the sum of all; he is the right, the pure meaning
and contents of the law. Whoso has Christ, has
rightly fulfilled the law. But to take away the law altogether, which sticks in nature, and is written in
our hearts and born in us, is a thing impossible
and against God. And whereas the law of nature is
somewhat darker, and speaks only of works, therefore, Moses and the Holy Ghost more clearly declare
and expound it, by naming those works which God
will have us to do, and to leave undone. Hence
Christ also says: "I am not come to destroy the
law." Worldly people would willingly give him
royal entertainment who could bring this to pass,
and make out that Moses, through Christ, is quite
taken away. O, then we should quickly see what a
fine kind of life there would be in the world! But
God forbid, and keep us from such errors, and suffer us not to live to see the same.

· 241 ·

We must preach the law for the sake of the evil
and wicked, but for the most part it lights upon the
good and godly, who, although they need it not,
except so far as may concern the old Adam, flesh

and blood, yet accept it. The preaching of the gospel we must have for the sake of the good and godly, yet it falls among the wicked and ungodly, who take it to themselves, whereas it profits them not; for they abuse it, and are thereby made confident. It is even as when it rains in the water or on a desert wilderness, and, meantime, the good pastures and grounds are parched and dried up. The ungodly out of the gospel suck only a carnal freedom, and become worse thereby; therefore, not the gospel, but the law belongs to them. Even as when my little son John offends, if then I should not whip him, but call him to the table to me, and give him sugar-plums, thereby I should make him worse, yea, quite spoil him.

The gospel is like a fresh, mild, and cool air in the extreme heat of summer, a solace and comfort in the anguish of the conscience. But as this heat proceeds from the rays of the sun, so likewise the terrifying of the conscience must proceed from the preaching of the law, to the end we may know that we have offended against the laws of God.

Now, when the mind is refreshed and quickened again by the cool air of the gospel, then we must not be idle, lie down and sleep. That is, when our consciences are settled in peace, quieted and comforted through God's Spirit, we must prove our faith by such good works as God has commanded. But so long as we live in this vale of misery, we shall be plagued and vexed with flies, with beetles, and vermin, that is, with the devil, the world, and our own flesh; yet we must press through, and not suffer ourselves to recoil.

· 242 ·

In what darkness, unbelief, traditions, and ordinances of men we have lived, and in how many conflicts of the conscience we have been ensnared, confounded, and captivated under Popedom, is testified by the books of the papists, and by many people now living. From all which snares and horrors we are now delivered and freed by Jesus Christ and his gospel, and are called to the true righteousness of faith; insomuch that with good and peaceable consciences we now believe in God the Father, we trust in him, and have just cause to boast that we have sure and certain remission of our sins through the death of Christ Jesus, dearly bought and purchased. Who can sufficiently extol these treasures of the conscience, which everywhere are spread abroad, offered and presented merely by grace? We are now conquerors of sin, of the law, of death, and of the devil; freed and delivered from all human traditions. If we would but consider the tyranny of auricular confession one of the least things we have escaped from, we could not show ourselves sufficiently thankful to God for loosing us out of that one snare. When Popedom stood and flourished among us, then every king would willingly have given ten hundred thousand guilders, a prince one hundred thousand, a nobleman one thousand, a gentleman one hundred, a citizen or countryman twenty or ten, to have been freed from that tyranny. But now seeing such freedom is obtained for nothing, by grace, it is not much regarded, neither give we thanks to God for it.

· 243 ·

Augustin pictured the strength, office, and operation of the law, by a very fit similitude, to show, that it discovers our sins, and God's wrath against sin, and places them in our sight. "The law," says he, "is not in fault, but our evil and wicked nature; even as a heap of lime is still and quiet, until water be poured thereon, but then it begins to smoke and burn, not from the fault of the water, but from the nature and kind of the lime, which will not endure water; whereas, if oil, instead, be poured upon it, then it lies still, and burns not; even so it is with the law and the gospel."

· 244 ·

On this matter of the righteousness of the law, St. Paul thoroughly bestirred himself against God's professing people, as in Rom. ix, x., xi., he strives with powerful, well-based arguments; it produced him much sorrow of heart.

The Jews' argument was this: Paul kept the law at Jerusalem, therefore, said they, we must also keep it. Answer: True, Paul for a certain time kept the law, by reason of the weak, to win them; but, in this our time, it is not so, and agrees not in any way therewith; as the ancient father well said: Distinguish times, and we may easily reconcile the Scriptures together.

OF JUSTIFICATION

· 245 ·

ALL men, indeed, are not alike strong, so that in some, many faults, weaknesses, and offences, are found; but these do not hinder them of sanctification, if they sin not of evil purpose and premeditation, but only out of weakness. For a Christian, indeed, feels the lusts of the flesh, but he resists them, and they have not dominion over him; and although, now and then, he stumbles and falls into sin, yet it is forgiven him, when he rises again, and holds on to Christ, who will not "That the lost sheep be hunted away, but be sought after."

· 246 ·

Why do Christians make use of their natural wisdom and understanding, seeing it must be set aside in matters of faith, as not only not understanding them, but also as striving against them.

Answer: The natural wisdom of a human creature in matters of faith, until he be regenerate and born anew, is altogether darkness, knowing nothing in divine cases. But in a faithful person, regenerate and enlightened by the Holy Spirit, through the Word, it is a fair and glorious instrument, and work of God: for even as all God's gifts, natural instruments, and expert faculties, are hurtful to the ungodly, even so are they wholesome and saving to the good and godly.

The understanding, through faith, receives life

from faith; that which was dead, is made alive again; like as our bodies, in light day, when it is clear and bright, are better disposed, rise, move, walk, &c., more readily and safely than they do in the dark night, so it is with human reason, which strives not against faith, when enlightened, but rather furthers and advances it.

So the tongue, which before blasphemed God, now lauds, extols, and praises God and his grace, as my tongue, now it is enlightened, is now another manner of tongue than it was in Popedom; a regeneration done by the Holy Ghost through the Word.

A sanctified and upright Christian says: My wife, my children, my art, my wisdom, my money and wealth, help and avail me nothing in heaven; yet I cast them not away nor reject them when God bestows such benefits upon me, but part and separate the substance from the vanity and foolery which cleave thereunto. Gold is and remains gold as well when a strumpet carries it about her, as when 'tis with an honest, good, and godly woman. The body of a strumpet is even as well God's creature, as the body of an honest matron. In this manner ought we to part and separate vanity and folly from the thing and substance, or from the creature given and God who created it.

· 247 ·

Upright and faithful Christians ever think they are not faithful, nor believe as they ought; and therefore they constantly strive, wrestle, and are diligent to keep and to increase faith, as good workmen always see that something is wanting in their workmanship. But the botchers think that nothing is wanting in what they do, but that everything is well and complete. Like as the Jews conceive they have the ten commandments at their fingers' end, whereas, in truth, they neither learn nor regard them.

· 248 ·

Truly it is held for presumption in a human creature that he dare boast of his own proper righteousness of faith; 'tis a hard matter for a man to say: I am the child of God, and am comforted and solaced through the immeasurable grace and mercy of my heavenly Father. To do this from the heart, is not in every man's power. Therefore no man is able to teach pure and aright touching faith, nor

to reject the righteousness of works, without sound
practice and experience. St. Paul was well exercised
in this art; he speaks more vilely of the law than
any arch heretic can speak of the sacrament of
the altar, of baptism, or than the Jews have spoken
thereof; for he names the law, the ministration of
death, the ministration of sin, and the ministration
of condemnation; yea, he holds all the works of the
law, and what the law requires, without Christ, dangerous and hurtful, which Moses, if he had then
lived, would doubtless have taken very ill at Paul's
hands. It was, according to human reason, spoken
too scornfully.

· 249 ·

Faith and hope are variously distinguishable.
And, first, in regard of the subject, wherein everything subsists: faith consists in a person's understanding, hope in the will; these two cannot be
separated; they are like the two cherubim over the
mercy-seat.

Secondly, in regard of the office: faith indites,
distinguishes, and teaches, and is the knowledge
and acknowledgment; hope admonishes, awakens,
hears, expects, and suffers.

Thirdly, in regard to the object: faith looks to the

word or promise, which is truth; but hope to that
which the Word promises, which is the good or
benefit.

Fourthly, in regard of order in degree: faith is
first, and before all adversities and troubles, and is
the beginning of life, Heb. xi. But hope follows after,
and springs up in trouble, Rom. v.

Fifthly, by reason of the contrariety: faith fights
against errors and heresies; it proves and judges
spirits and doctrines. But hope strives against troubles and vexations, and among the evil it expects
good.

Faith, in divinity, is the wisdom and providence,
and belongs to the doctrine. But hope is the courage
and joyfulness in divinity, and pertains to admonition. Faith is the *dialectica,* for it is altogether
prudence and wisdom; hope is the *rhetorica,* an elevation of the heart and mind. As wisdom without
courage is futile, even so faith without hope is
nothing worth; for hope endures and overcomes
misfortune and evil. And as a joyous valour without understanding is but rashness, so hope without
faith is spiritual presumption. Faith is the key to
the sacred Scriptures, the right *Cabala* or exposition, which one receives of tradition, as the prophets
left this doctrine to their disciples. 'Tis said St.

Peter wept whenever he thought of the gentleness with which Jesus taught. Faith is given from one to another, and remains continually in one school. Faith is not a quality, as the schoolmen say, but a gift of God.

· 250 ·

Everything that is done in the world is done by hope. No husbandman would sow one grain of corn, if he hoped not it would grow up and become seed; no bachelor would marry a wife, if he hoped not to have children; no merchant or tradesman would set himself to work, if he did not hope to reap benefit thereby, &c. How much more, then, does hope urge us on to everlasting life and salvation?

· 251 ·

Faith's substance is our will; its manner is, that we take hold on Christ by divine instinct; its final cause and fruit, that it purifies the heart, makes us children of God, and brings with it the remission of sins.

· 252 ·

Adam received the promise of the woman's seed ere he had done any work or sacrifice, to the end

God's truth might stand fast—namely, that we are justified before God altogether without works, and obtain forgiveness of sins merely by grace. Whoso is able to believe this well and steadfastly, is a doctor above all the doctors in the world.

· 253 ·

Faith is not only necessary, that thereby the ungodly may become justified and saved before God, and their hearts be settled in peace, but it is necessary in every other respect. St. Paul says: "Now that we are justified by faith, we have peace with God through our Lord Jesus Christ."

· 254 ·

Joseph of Arimathea had a faith in Christ, like as the apostles had; he thought Christ would have been a worldly and temporal potentate; therefore he took care of him as of a good friend, and buried him honourably. He believed not that Christ should rise again from death, and become a spiritual and everlasting king.

· 255 ·

When Abraham shall rise again, at the last day,

then he will chide us for our unbelief, and will say: I had not the hundredth part of the promises which ye have, and yet I believed. That example of Abraham exceeds all human natural reason, who, overcoming the paternal love he bore towards his only son Isaac, was all obedient to God, and, against the law of nature, would have sacrificed that son. What, for the space of three days, he felt in his breast, how his heart yearned and panted, what hesitations and trials he had, cannot be expressed.

· 256 ·

All heretics have continually failed in this one point, that they do not rightly understand or know the article of justification. If we had not this article certain and clear, it were impossible we could criticise the pope's false doctrine of indulgences and other abominable errors, much less be able to overcome greater spiritual errors and vexations. If we only permit Christ to be our Saviour, then we have won, for he is the only girdle which clasps the whole body together, as St. Paul excellently teaches.

If we look to the spiritual birth and substance of a true Christian, we shall soon extinguish all deserts of good works; for they serve us to no use, neither to purchase sanctification, nor to deliver us from sin, death, devil, or hell.

Little children are saved only by faith without any good works; therefore faith alone justifies. If God's power be able to effect that in one, then he is also able to accomplish it in all; for the power of the child effects it not, but the power of faith; neither is it done through the child's weakness or disability; for then that weakness would be merit of itself, or equivalent to merit. It is a mischievous thing that we miserable, sinful wretches will upbraid God, and hit him in the teeth with our works, and think thereby to be justified before him; but God will not allow it.

· 257 ·

This article, how we are saved, is the chief of the whole Christian doctrine, to which all divine disputations must be directed. All the prophets were chiefly engaged upon it, and sometimes much perplexed about it. For when this article is kept fast and sure by a constant faith, then all other articles draw on softly after, as that of the Holy Trinity, &c. God has declared no article so plainly and openly as this, that we are saved only by Christ;

though he speaks much of the Holy Trinity, yet he
dwells continually upon this article of the salvation
of our souls; other articles are of great weight, but
this surpasses all.

· 258 ·

A capuchin says: wear a grey coat and a hood,
a rope round thy body, and sandals on thy feet. A
cordelier says: put on a black hood; an ordinary
papist says: do this or that work, hear mass, pray,
fast, give alms, &c. But a true Christian says: I am
justified and saved only by faith in Christ, without
any works or merits of my own; compare these together, and judge which is the true righteousness.

· 259 ·

Christ says: "The spirit is willing, but the flesh
is weak:" St. Paul also says: the spirit willingly
would give itself wholly unto God, would trust in
him, and be obedient; but natural reason and understanding, flesh and blood, resist and will not go
forward. Therefore our Lord God must needs have
patience and bear with us. God will not put out the
glimmering flax; the faithful have as yet but only
the first fruits of the spirit; they have not the ful-
filling, but the tenth.

· 260 ·

I well understand that St. Paul was also weak in faith, whence he boasted, and said: "I am a servant of God, and an apostle of Jesus Christ." An angel stood by him at sea, and comforted him, and when he came to Rome, he was comforted as he saw the brethren come out to meet him. Hereby we see what the communion and company does of such as fear God. The Lord commanded the disciples to remain together in one place, before they received the Holy Ghost, and to comfort one another; for Christ well knew that adversaries would assault them.

· 261 ·

A Christian must be well armed, grounded, and furnished with sentences out of God's word, that so he may stand and defend religion and himself against the devil, in case he should be asked to embrace another doctrine.

· 262 ·

When at the last day we shall live again, we shall blush for shame, and say to ourselves: "Fie on thee, in that thou hast not been more courageous, bold, and strong to believe in Christ, and to endure all manner of adversities, crosses, and persecutions, seeing his glory is so great. If I were now in the world, I would not stick to suffer ten thousand times more."

· 263 ·

Although a man knew, and could do as much as the angels in heaven, yet all this would not make him a Christian, unless he knew Christ and believed in him. God says: "Let not the wise man glory in his wisdom, neither let the mighty man glory in his might; let not the rich man glory in his riches: but let him that glorieth, glory in this, that he understandeth and knoweth me, that I am the Lord, which doth exercise loving-kindness, judgment, and righteousness," &c.

· 264 ·

As to ceremonies and ordinances, the kingdom of love must have precedence and government, and not tyranny. It must be a willing, not a halter love; it must altogether be directed and construed for the good and profit of the neighbour; and the greater he that governs, the more he ought to serve according to love.

· 265 ·

The love toward our neighbours must be like the pure and chaste love between bride and bridegroom, where all faults are connived at and borne with, and only the virtues regarded.

· 266 ·

Believest thou? then thou wilt speak boldly. Speakest thou boldly? then thou must suffer. Sufferest thou? then thou shalt be comforted. For faith, the confession thereof, and the cross, follow one upon another.

· 267 ·

Give and it shall be given unto you: this is a fine maxim, and makes people poor and rich; it is that which maintains my house. I would not boast, but I well know what I give away in the year. If my gracious lord and master, the prince elector, should give a gentleman two thousand florins, this should hardly answer to the cost of my housekeeping for one year; and yet I have but three hundred florins a year, but God blesses these, and makes them suffice.

There is in Austria a monastery, which, in former times, was very rich, and remained rich so long as

it was charitable to the poor; but when it ceased to
give, then it became indigent, and is so to this
day. Not long since, a poor man went there and
solicited alms, which was denied him; he demanded
the cause why they refused to give for God's sake?
The porter of the monastery answered: We are become poor; whereupon the mendicant said: The
cause of your poverty is this: ye had formerly in
this monastery two brethren, the one named *Date*
(give), and the other *Dabitur* (it shall be given
you). The former ye thrust out; the other went
away of himself.

We are bound to help one's neighbour three manner of ways—with giving, lending, and selling. But
no man gives; every one scrapes and claws all to
himself; each would willingly steal, but give nothing, and lend but upon usury. No man sells unless
he can over-reach his neighbour; therefore is
Dabitur gone, and our Lord God will bless us no
more so richly. Beloved, he that desires to have anything, must also give:﹒a liberal hand was never in
want, or empty.

· 268 ·

Desert is a work nowhere to be found, for Christ
gives a reward by reason of the promise. If the

prince elector should say to me: Come to the court, and I will give thee one hundred florins, I perform a work in going to the court, yet I receive not the gift by reason of my work in going thither, but by reason of the promise the prince made me.

· 269 ·

I marvel at the madness and bitterness of Wetzell, in undertaking to write so much against the Protestants, assailing us without rhyme or reason, and, as we say, getting a case out of a hedge; as where he rages against this principle of ours, that the works and acts of a farmer, husbandman, or any other good and godly Christian, if done in faith, are far more precious in the sight of God, than all the works of monks, friars, nuns, &c. This poor, ignorant fellow gets very angry against us, regarding not the works which God has commanded and imposed upon each man in his vocation, state, and calling. He heeds only superstitious practices, devised for show and effect, which God neither commands nor approves of.

St. Paul, in his epistles, wrote of good works and virtues more energetically and truthfully than all the philosophers; for he extols highly the works of godly Christians, in their respective vocations and callings. Let Wetzell know that David's wars and battles were more pleasing to God than the fastings and prayings even of the holiest of the old monks, setting aside altogether the works of the monks of our time, which are simply ridiculous.

· 270 ·

I never work better than when I am inspired by anger; when I am angry, I can write, pray, and preach well, for then my whole temperament is quickened, my understanding sharpened, and all mundane vexations and temptations depart.

· 271 ·

Dr. Justus Jonas asked me if the thoughts and words of the prophet Jeremiah were Christianlike, when he cursed the day of his birth. I said: We must now and then wake up our Lord God with such words. Jeremiah had cause to murmur in this way. Did not our Saviour Christ say: "O faithless and perverse generation! How long shall I be with you, and suffer you?" Moses also took God in hand, where he said: "Wherefore hast thou afflicted thy servant? Have I conceived all this people? Have I begotten them?"

· 272 ·

A man must needs be plunged in bitter affliction when in his heart he means good, and yet is not regarded. I can never get rid of these cogitations, wishing I had never begun this business with the pope. So, too, I desire myself rather dead than to hear or see God's Word and his servants contemned; but 'tis the frailty of our nature to be thus discouraged.

They who condemn the movement of anger against antagonists, are theologians who deal in mere speculations; they play with words, and occupy themselves with subtleties, but when they are aroused, and take a real interest in the matter, they are touched sensibly.

· 273 ·

"In quietness and in confidence shall be your strength." This sentence I expounded thus: If thou intendest to vanquish the greatest, the most abominable and wickedest enemy, who is able to do thee mischief both in body and soul, and against whom thou preparest all sorts of weapons, but canst not overcome; then know that there is a sweet and loving physical herb to serve thee, named *Patientia*.

Thou wilt say: How may I attain this physic? Take unto thee faith, which says: no creature can do me mischief without the will of God. In case thou receivest hurt and mischief by thine enemy, this is done by the sweet and gracious will of God, in such sort that the enemy hurts himself a thousand times more than he does thee. Hence flows unto me, a Christian, the love which says: I will, instead of the evil which mine enemy does unto me, do him all the good I can; I will heap coals of fire upon his head. This is the Christian armour and weapon, wherewith to beat and overcome those enemies that seem to be like huge mountains. In a word, love teaches to suffer and endure all things.

· 274 ·

A certain honest and God-forbearing man at Wittenberg, told me, that though he lived peacefully with every one, hurt no man, was ever quiet, yet many people were enemies unto him. I comforted him in this manner: Arm thyself with patience, and be not angry though they hate thee; what offence, I pray, do we give the devil? What ails him to be so great an enemy unto us? only because he has not that which God has; I know no other cause of his vehement hatred towards us. If God give thee to eat, eat; if he cause thee to fast, be resigned thereto; gives he thee honours? take them; hurt or shame? endure it; casts he thee into prison? murmur not; will he make thee a king? obey him; casts he thee down again? heed it not.

· 275 ·

Patience is the most excellent of the virtues, and, in Sacred Writ, highly praised and recommended by the Holy Ghost. The learned heathen philosophers applaud it, but they do not know its genuine basis, being without the assistance of God. Epictetus, the wise and judicious Greek, said very well: "Suffer and abstain."

· 276 ·

It was the custom of old, in burying the dead, to lay their heads towards the sun-rising, by reason of a spiritual mystery and signification therein manifested; but this was not an enforced law. So all laws and ceremonies should be free in the church, and not be done on compulsion, being things which neither justify nor condemn in the

sight of God, but are observed merely for the sake
of orderly discipline.

· 277 ·

The righteousness of works and hypocrisy, are
the most mischievous diseases born in us, and not
easily expelled, especially when they are confirmed
and settled upon us by use and practice; for all
mankind will have dealings with Almighty God, and
dispute with him, according to their human natural understanding, and will make satisfaction to
God for their sins, with their own strength and
self-chosen works. For my part, I have so often
deceived our Lord God by promising to be upright
and good, that I will promise no more, but will
only pray for a happy hour, when it shall please
God to make me good.

· 278 ·

A popish priest once argued with me in this manner: Evil works are damned, therefore good works
justify. I answered: This your argument is nothing
worth; it concludes not *ratione contrariorum;* the
things are not in connection; evil works are evil
in complete measure, because they proceed from a
heart that is altogether spoiled and evil; but good

works, yea, even in an upright Christian, are incompletely good; for they proceed out of a weak obedience but little recovered and restored. Whoso can say from his heart: I am a sinner, but God is righteous; and who, at the point of death, from his heart can say: Lord Jesus Christ, I commit my spirit into thy hands, may assure himself of true righteousness, and that he is not of the number of those that blaspheme God, in relying upon their own works and righteousness.

OF PRAYER

· 279 ·

NONE can believe how powerful prayer is, and what it is able to effect, but those who have learned it by experience.

It is a great matter when in extreme need, to take hold on prayer. I know, whenever I have earnestly prayed, I have been amply heard, and have obtained more than I prayed for; God, indeed, sometimes delayed, but at last he came.

Ecclesiasticus says: "The prayer of a good and godly Christian availeth more to health, than the physician's physic."

O how great a thing, how marvellous, a godly Christian's prayer is! how powerful with God; that a poor human creature should speak with God's high Majesty in heaven, and not be affrighted, but, on the contrary, know that God smiles upon him for Christ's sake, his dearly beloved Son. The heart and conscience, in this act of praying, must not fly and recoil backwards by reason of our sins and unworthiness, or stand in doubt, or be scared away. We must not do as the Bavarian did, who, with great devotion, called upon St. Leonard, an idol set up in a church in Bavaria, behind which idol stood one who answered the Bavarian, and said: Fie on thee, Bavarian; and in that sort often repulsed and would not hear him, till at last, the Bavarian went away, and said: Fie on thee, Leonard.

When we pray, we must not let it come to: Fie upon thee; but certainly hold and believe, that we are already heard in that for which we pray, with faith in Christ. Therefore the ancients ably defined prayer an *Ascensus mentis ad Deum*, a climbing up of the heart unto God.

· 280 ·

Our Saviour Christ as excellently as briefly comprehends in the Lord's prayer all things needful and necessary. Except under troubles, trials, and vexations, prayer cannot rightly be made. God says: "Call on me in the time of trouble;" without trouble it is only a bald prattling, and not from the heart; 'tis a common saying: "Need teaches to pray." And though the papists say that God well understands all the words of those that pray, yet St. Bernard is far of another opinion, who says: God hears not the words of one that prays, unless he that prays first hears them himself. The pope is a mere tormentor of the conscience. The assemblies of his greased crew, in prayer, were altogether like the croaking of frogs, which edified nothing at all; mere sophistry and deceit, fruitless and unprofitable. Prayer is a strong wall and fortress of the church; it is a godly Christian's weapon, which no man knows or finds, but only he who has the spirit of grace and of prayer.

The three first petitions in our Lord's prayer comprehend such great and celestial things, that no heart is able to search them out. The fourth contains the whole policy and economy of temporal

and house government, and all things necessary for
this life. The fifth fights against our own evil consciences, and against original and actual sins, which
trouble them. Truly that prayer was penned by wisdom itself; none but God could have done it.

· 281 ·

Prayer in Popedom is mere tongue-threshing;
not prayer, but a work of obedience. Thence a confused sea of *Horæ Canonicæ*, the howling and bab-
bling in cells and monasteries, where they read and
sing the psalms and collects, without any spiritual
devotion, understanding neither the words, sentences, nor meaning.

How I tormented myself with those *Horæ Canonicæ* before the gospel came, which by reason of
much business I often intermitted, I cannot express. On the Saturdays, I used to lock myself up
in my cell, and accomplish what the whole week I
had neglected. But at last I was troubled with so
many affairs, that I was fain often to omit also
my Saturday's devotions. At length, when I saw
that Amsdorf and others derided such devotion,
then I quite left it off.

From this great torment we are now delivered by
the gospel. Though I had done no more but only

freed people from that torment, they might well give
me thanks for it.

· 282 ·

We cannot pray without faith in Christ the Mediator. Turks, Jews, and papists may repeat the words
of prayer, but they cannot pray. And although the
Apostles were taught this Lord's prayer by Christ,
and prayed often, yet they prayed not as they should
have prayed; for Christ says: "Hitherto ye have
not prayed in my name;" whereas, doubtless, they
had prayed much, speaking the words. But when
the Holy Ghost came, then they prayed aright in
the name of Christ. If praying and reading of
prayer be but only a bare work, as the papists hold,
then the righteousness of the law is nothing worth.
The upright prayer of a godly Christian is a strong
hedge, as God himself says: "And I sought for a
man among them that should make up the hedge,
and stand in the gap before me for the land, that
I should not destroy it, but I found none."

· 283 ·

When Moses, with the children of Israel, came to
the Red Sea, then he cried with trembling and
quaking; yet he opened not his mouth, neither was

his voice heard on earth by the people; doubtless,
he cried and sighed in his heart, and said: Ah,
Lord God! what course shall I now take? Which
way shall I now turn myself? How am I come to
this strait? No help or counsel can save us; before
us is the sea; behind us are our enemies the Egyp-
tians; on both sides high and huge mountains; I
am the cause that all this people shall now be destroyed. Then answered God, and said: "Wherefore criest thou unto me?" as if God should say:
What an alarum dost thou make, that the whole
heavens ring! Human reason is not able to search
this passage out. The way through the Red Sea is
full as broad and wide, if not wider, than Wittenberg lies from Coburg, that so, doubtless, the people
were constrained in the night season to rest and to
eat therein; for six hundred thousand men, besides
women and children, would require a good time to
pass through, though they went one hundred and
fifty abreast.

· 284 ·

It is impossible that God should not hear the
prayers which with faith are made in Christ, though
he give not according to the measure, manner, and
time we dictate, for he will not be tied. In such sort

dealt God with the mother of St. Augustin; she prayed to God that her son might be converted, but as yet it would not be; then she ran to the learned, intreating them to persuade and advise him thereunto. She propounded unto him a marriage with a Christian virgin, that thereby he might be drawn and brought to the Christian faith, but all would not do as yet. But when our Lord God came thereto, he came to purpose, and made of him such an Augustin, that he became a great light to the church. St. James says: "Pray one for another, for the prayer of the righteous availeth much." Prayer is a powerful thing; for God has bound and tied himself thereunto.

· 285 ·

Christ gave the Lord's prayer according to the ideas of the Jews—that is, he directed it only to the Father, whereas they that pray, should pray as though they were to be heard for the Son's sake. This was because Christ would not be praised before his death.

· 286 ·

Justus Jonas asked Luther if these sentences in Scripture did not contradict each other; where God says to Abraham: "If I find ten in Sodom, I will not destroy it;" and where Ezekiel says: "Though these three men, Noah, Daniel, and Job, were in it, yet would I not hear," &c.; and where Jeremiah says: "Therefore pray not thou for this people." Luther answered: No, they are not against one another; for in Ezekiel it was forbidden them to pray, but it was not so with Abraham. Therefore we must have regard to the word; when God says: thou shalt not pray, then we may well cease.

• 287 •

When governors and rulers are enemies to God's Word, then our duty is to depart, to sell and forsake all we have, to fly from one place to another, as Christ commands. We must make for ourselves no tumults, by reason of the gospel, but suffer all things.

• 288 •

Upright Christians pray without ceasing; though they pray not always with their mouths, yet their hearts pray continually, sleeping and waking; for the sigh of a true Christian is a prayer. As the Psalm saith: "Because of the deep sighing of the poor, I will up, saith the Lord," &c. In like manner a true Christian always carries the cross, though he feel it not always.

· 289 ·

The Lord's prayer binds the people together, and knits them one to another, so that one prays for another, and together one with another; and it is so strong and powerful that it even drives away the fear of death.

· 290 ·

Prayer preserves the church, and hitherto has done the best for the church; therefore we must continually pray. Hence Christ says: "Ask, and ye shall have; seek, and ye shall find; knock, and it shall be opened unto you."

First, when we are in trouble, he will have us to pray; for God often, as it were, hides himself, and will not hear; yea, will not suffer himself to be found. Then we must seek him; that is, we must continue in prayer. When we seek him, he often locks himself up, as it were, in a private chamber; if we intend to come in unto him, then we must knock, and when we have knocked once or twice, then he begins a little to hear. At last, when we make much knocking, then he opens, and says:

What will ye have? Lord, say we, we would have this or that; then, says he, Take it unto you. In such sort must we persist in praying, and waken God up.

OF BAPTISM

· 291 ·

THE ancient teachers ordained three sorts of baptizing; of water, of the Spirit, and of blood; these were observed in the church. The catechumens were baptized in water; others, that could not get such water-bathing, and nevertheless believed, were saved in and through the Holy Spirit, as Cornelius was saved, before he was baptized. The third sort were baptized in blood, that is, in martyrdom.

· 292 ·

Heaven is given unto me freely, for nothing. I have assurance hereof confirmed unto me by sealed covenants, that is, I am baptized, and frequent the sacrament of the Lord's Supper. Therefore I keep the bond safe and sure, lest the devil tear it in pieces; that is, I live and remain in God's fear, and pray daily unto him. God could not have given me better security of my salvation, and of the gospel, than by the death and passion of his only Son: when I believe that he overcame death, and died for me, and therewith behold the promise of the Father, then I have the bond complete. And when I have the seal of baptism and the Lord's Supper prefixed thereto, then I am well provided for.

· 293 ·

I was asked: when there is uncertainty, whether a person has been baptized or not, may he be baptized under a condition, as thus: If thou be not baptized, then I baptize thee? I answered: The church must exclude such baptizing, and not endure it, though there be a doubt of the previous baptizing of any person, yet he shall receive baptism, pure and simple, without any condition.

· 294 ·

If a woman that had murdered her child were absolved by me, and the crime were afterwards discovered publicly, and I were examined before the judge, I might not give witness in the matter—

we must make a difference between the church and
temporal government. She confessed not to me as
to a man, but to Christ, and if Christ keep silence
thereupon, it is my duty to keep silence also, and
to say: I know nothing of the matter thereof; if
Christ heard it, then may he speak of it; though,
meantime, I would privately say to the woman:
Thou wretch, do so no more. For, while I am not
the man to speak before the seat of justice, in temporal causes, in matters touching the conscience, I
ought to affright sinners with God's wrath against
sin, through the law. Such as acknowledge and confess their sins, I must lift up and comfort again,
by the preaching of the gospel. We will not be
drawn to their seats of justice, and markets of
hatred and dissension. We have hitherto protected
and maintained the jurisdiction and rights of the
church, and still will do so, yielding not in the least
to the temporal jurisdiction in causes belonging
to doctrine and consciences. Let them mind their
charge, wherewith they will find enough to do, and
leave ours to us, as Christ has commanded.

· 295 ·

Auricular confession was instituted only that people might give an account of their faith, and from

their hearts confess an earnest desire to receive the holy sacrament. We force no man thereunto.

· 296 ·

Christ gave the keys to the church for her comfort, and commanded her servants to deal therewith according to his direction, to bind the impenitent, and to absolve them that, repenting, acknowledge and confess their sins, are heartily sorry for them, and believe that God forgives them for Christ's sake.

· 297 ·

It was asked, did the Hussites well in administering the sacrament to young children, on the allegation that the graces of God apply equally to all human creatures. Dr. Luther replied: they were undoubtedly wrong, since young children need not the communion for their salvation; but still the innovation could not be regarded as a sin of the Hussites, since St. Cyprian, long ago, set them the example.

· 298 ·

Does he to whom the sacrament is administered by a heretic, really receive the sacrament? Yes, replied Dr. Luther: if he be ignorant that the person administering is a heretic. The sacramentarians reject the body of Christ; the anabaptists baptism, and therefore they cannot efficiently baptize; yet if a person apply to a sacramentarian, not knowing him as such, and receive from him the sacrament, himself believing it to be the veritable body of Christ, it is the veritable body of Christ that he actually receives.

· 299 ·

The anabaptists cavil as to how the salvation of man is to be effected by water. The simple answer is, that all things are possible to him who believes in God Almighty. If, indeed, a baker were to say to me: "This bread is a body, and this wine is blood," I should laugh at him incredulously. But when Jesus Christ, the Almighty God, taking in his hand bread and wine, tells me: "This is my body and my blood," then we must believe, for it is God who speaks—God who with a word created all things.

· 300 ·

It was asked whether, in a case of necessity, the father of a family might administer the Lord's supper to his children or servants. Dr. Luther replied: "By no means, for he is not called thereto, and they who are not called, may not preach, much less administer the sacrament. 'Twould lead to infinite disorder, for many people would then wholly dispense with the ministers of the church."

· 301 ·

When Jesus Christ directed his apostles to go and instruct and baptize all nations, he meant not that children should be excluded; the apostles were to baptize all the Gentiles, young or old, great or small. The baptism of children is distinctly enjoined in Mark x. 14: "The kingdom of God is of little children." We must not look at this text with the eyes of a calf, or of a cow vaguely gaping at a new gate, but do with it as at court we do with the prince's letters, read it and weigh it, and read it and weigh it again and again, with our most earnest attention.

· 302 ·

The papists say that 'twas Pope Melchiades baptized the emperor Constantine, but this is a fiction. The emperor Constantine was baptized at Nicomedia by Eusebius, bishop of that town, in the sixty-fifth year of his life, and the thirty-third of his reign.

· 303 ·

The anabaptists pretend that children, not as yet
having reason, ought not to receive baptism. I answer: That reason in no way contributes to faith.
Nay, in that children are destitute of reason, they
are all the more fit and proper recipients of baptism. For reason is the greatest enemy that faith
has: it never comes to the aid of spiritual things,
but—more frequently than not—struggles against
the Divine Word, treating with contempt all that
emanates from God. If God can communicate the
Holy Ghost to grown persons, he can, *à fortiori*,
communicate it to young children. Faith comes of
the Word of God, when this is heard; little children
hear that Word when they receive baptism, and
therewith they receive also faith.

· 304 ·

When, in a difficult labour, the arm or leg of the
child alone presents itself, we must not baptize that
limb, under the idea that thereby the infant can
receive baptism. Still less can it be pretended that
you baptize a child not yet come into the world, by
pouring water on the mother. The text of St. John
manifestly shows that such practices are prohibited

by Scripture: "Except a man be born again, he cannot see the kingdom of God." We must not, therefore, baptize a child until it has actually come into the world, whole and entire. When any difficulty occurs, those present must kneel and pray unto Christ, that he will deign to deliver the poor child and its mother from their sufferings, and they must do this in full confidence that the Lord will thereupon listen to the dictates of his merciful nature and wisdom. This prayer, offered up in faith, introduces the child to the Almighty, who himself has said: "Suffer little children to come unto me, for of such is the kingdom of God." We may rest assured that, under such circumstances, the child is not excluded from salvation, even though it die without having been regularly baptized. Should an infant, on coming into the world, be so extremely weak and feeble that there is manifest danger of its dying ere it can be carried to the church, then the women present should baptize it themselves, in the usual form. For this purpose, it is always desirable that the mother should have about her at least two or three persons, to attest that baptism has in this way been administered to the child, *ex necessitate.*

· 305 ·

Some one sent to know whether it was permissible
to use warm water in baptism? The Doctor replied:
"Tell the blockhead that water, warm or cold, is
water."

· 306 ·

In 1541, Doctor Menius asked Doctor Luther,
in what manner a Jew should be baptized? The
Doctor replied: You must fill a large tub with
water, and, having divested the Jew of his clothes,
cover him with a white garment. He must then sit
down in the tub, and you must baptize him quite
under the water. The ancients, when they were baptized, were attired in white, whence the first Sunday after Easter, which was peculiarly consecrated
to this ceremony, was called *dominica in albis*. This
garb was rendered the more suitable, from the circumstance that it was, as now, the custom to bury
people in a white shroud; and baptism, you know,
is an emblem of our death. I have no doubt that
when Jesus was baptized in the river Jordan, he
was attired in a white robe. If a Jew, not converted
at heart, were to ask baptism at my hands, I would
take him on to the bridge, tie a stone round his
neck, and hurl him into the river; for these wretches

are wont to make a jest of our religion. Yet, after all, water and the Divine Word being the essence of baptism, a Jew, or any other, would be none the less validly baptized, that his own feelings and intentions were not the result of faith.

OF THE SACRAMENT OF THE LORD'S SUPPER

· 307 ·

THE blindness of the papists is great and mischievous; for they will neither believe the gospel nor yield thereunto, but boast of the church, and say: She has power to alter, and to do what she pleases; for, say they, Christ gave his body to his disciples in the evening after supper; but we receive it fasting, therefore we may, according to the church's ordinance, detain the cup from the laity. The ignorant wretches are not able to distinguish between the cup, which pertains to the substance of the sacrament, and fasting, which is an accidental, carnal thing, of no weight at all. The one has God's express word and command, the other consists in our will and choice. We urge the one, because God has commanded it; the other we leave to the election of the will, though we better like it to be received fasting, out of honour and reverence.

· 308 ·

It is a wonder how Satan brought into the church, and ordained, but one kind of the sacrament to be received. I cannot call to mind that ever I read how, whence, or for what cause it was so altered. It was first so ordained in the council of Constance, where nothing, however, is pleaded but only the custom.

· 309 ·

The papists highly boast of their power and authority, which they would willingly confirm with this argument: the apostles altered baptism; therefore, say they, the bishops have power to alter the sacrament of the Lord's supper. I answer: admit that the apostles altered something; yet there is a great difference between an apostle and a bishop; an apostle was called immediately by God with gifts of the Holy Ghost; but a bishop is a person selected by man, to preach God's word, and ordain servants of the church in certain places. So, though the apostles had this power and authority, yet the bishops have not. Although Elijah slew Baal's priests and the false prophets, it is not permitted that every priest shall do the like. Hence St. Paul makes this difference: "Some hath he given to be apostles, some teachers, some to be pastors and ministers," &c. Among the apostles was no supremacy or ruling; none was greater or higher in office than another; they were all equal, the one with the other. The definition as to the supremacy and rule of St. Peter above other bishops is false; it reaches further than they define it; they conclude thus: the pope's power and authority is the highest; he may ordain servants, alter kingdoms and governments, depose some emperors and kings, and enthrone others. But we are in nowise to allow of such definitions; for every definition must be direct and proper, set down plain and clear; so that neither more nor less may in the definition be contained, than that which is described and defined.

· 310 ·

They that as yet are not well informed, but stand

in doubt, touching the institution of the sacrament, may receive it under one kind; but those that are certain thereof, and yet receive it under one kind, act wrongfully and against their consciences.

· 311 ·

What signifies it to dispute and wrangle about the abominable idolatry of elevating the sacrament on high to show it to the people, which has no approbation of the Fathers, and was introduced only to confirm the errors touching the worship thereof, as though bread and wine lost their substance, and retained only the form, smell, taste. This the papists call transubstantiation, and darken the right use of the sacrament; whereas, even in Popedom, at Milan, from Ambrose's time to the present day, they never held or observed in the mass either canon or elevation, or the *Dominus vobiscum*.

· 312 ·

The elevation of the sacrament was taken out of the Old Testament; the Jews observed two forms, the one called *Thruma*, the other *Trumpha*; *Thruma* was when they took an offering out of a basket, and lifted it up above them (like as they now lift up the oblate), and showed the same to our Lord God,

after which they either burned or ate it: *Trumpha,*
was an offering which they lifted not up above
them, but showed it towards the four corners of
the world, as the papists, in the mass, make crosses,
and other apish toys, towards the four corners of
the world.

When I first began to celebrate mass in Popedom,
and to make such crossings with marvellous twist-
ings of the fingers, and could not rightly hit the
way, I said: "Mary, God's mother, how am I
plagued with the mass, and especially with the
crossings." Ah, Lord God! we were in those times
poor plagued people, and yet it was nothing but
mere idolatry. They terrified some in such sort with
the words of consecration, especially good and
godly men who meant seriously, that they trembled
and quaked at the pronouncing of these words:
Hoc est corpus meum, for they were to pronounce
them, *sine ullâ hesitatione;* he that stammered, or
left out but one word, committed a great sin. Moreover, the words were to be spoken, without any ab-
straction of thought, in such a way, that only he
must hear them that spake them, and none of the
people standing by. Such an honest friar was I fifteen years together; the Lord of his mercy forgive
me. The elevation is utterly to be rejected by rea-

son of the adoring thereof. Some churches, seeing we have put down the elevation, have followed us therein, which gives me great satisfaction.

· 313 ·

The operative cause of the sacrament is the word and institution of Christ, who ordained it. The substance is bread and wine, prefiguring the true body and blood of Christ, which is spiritually received by faith. The final cause of instituting the same, is the benefit and the fruit, the strengthening of our faith, not doubting that Christ's body and blood were given and shed for us, and that our sins by Christ's death certainly are forgiven.

· 314 ·

Question was made touching the words "given for you," whether they were to be understood of the present administering, when the sacrament is distributed, or of when it was offered and accomplished on the cross? I said: I like it best when they are understood of the present administering, although they may be understood as fulfilled on the cross; it matters not that Christ says: "Which is given for you," instead of: "Which shall be given for you:" for Christ is *Hodie et Heri,* to-day and yesterday. I am, says Christ, he that doeth it. Therefore, I approve that *Datur* be understood in such manner, that it show the use of the work. It was likewise asked, whether honour and reverence were to be shown to the sacrament? I said: When I am at the altar, and receive the sacrament, I bow my knees in honour thereof; but in bed I receive it lying.

· 315 ·

They that do not hold the sacrament as Christ instituted it, have no sacrament. All papists do not, therefore they have no sacrament; for they receive not the sacrament, but offer it. Moreover, they administer but one kind, contrary to Christ's institution and command. The sacrament is God's work and ordinance, and not man's. The papists err in attributing to the sacrament, that it justifies, *ex opere operato,* when the work is fulfilled.

· 316 ·

These words, "Drink ye all of it," concern, say the papists, only the priests. Then these words must also concern only the priests, where Christ says: "Ye are clean, but not all," that is, all the priests.

OF THE CHURCH

· 317 ·

THE true church is an assembly or congregation depending on that which does not appear, nor may be comprehended in the mind, namely, God's Word; what that says, they believe without addition, giving God the honour.

· 318 ·

We tell our Lord God plainly, that if he will have his church, he must maintain and defend it; for we can neither uphold nor protect it; if we could, indeed, we should become the proudest asses under heaven. But God says: I say it, I do it: it is God only that speaks and does what he pleases; he does nothing according to the fancies of the ungodly, or which they hold for upright and good.

· 319 ·

The great and worldly-wise people take offence at the poor and mean form of our church, which is subject to many infirmities, transgressions, and sects, wherewith she is plagued; for they say the church should be altogether pure, holy, blameless, God's dove, &c. And the church, in the eyes and sight of God, has such an esteem; but in the eyes and sight of the world, she is like unto her bridegroom, Christ Jesus, torn, spit on, derided, and crucified.

The similitude of the upright and true church and of Christ, is a poor silly sheep; but the similitude of the false and hypocritical church, is a serpent, an adder.

· 320 ·

Where God's word is purely taught, there is also the upright and true church; for the true church is supported by the Holy Ghost, not by succession of inheritance. It does not follow, though St. Peter had been bishop at Rome, and at the same time Christian communion had been at Rome, that therefore, the pope and the Romish church are true; for if that should be of value or conclusive, then they must needs confess that Caiaphas, Annas, and the Sadducees were also the true church; for they boasted that they were descended from Aaron.

· 321 ·

It is impossible for the Christian and true church

to subsist without the shedding of blood, for her adversary, the devil, is a liar and a murderer. The church grows and increases through blood; she is sprinkled with blood; she is spoiled and bereaved of her blood; when human creatures will reform the church, then it costs blood.

· 322 ·

The form and aspect of the world is like a paradise; but the true Christian church, in the eye of the world, is foul, deformed, and offensive; yet, nevertheless, in the sight of God, she is precious, beloved, and highly esteemed. Aaron, the high-priest, appeared gloriously in the temple, with his ornaments and rich attire, with odoriferous and sweet-smelling perfumes; but Christ appeared most mean and lowly.

Wherefore I am not troubled that the world esteems the church so meanly; what care I that the usurers, the nobility, gentry, citizens, country-people, covetous men, and drunkards, contemn and esteem me as dirt? In due time, I will esteem them as little. We must not suffer ourselves to be received or troubled as to what the world thinks of us. To please the good is our virtue.

· 323 ·

The church is misery on earth, first, that we may keep in mind we are banished servants, and exiled out of Paradise for Adam's sake. Secondly, that we may always remember the misery of the Son of God, who, for our sake, was made man, walked in this vale of misery, suffered for us, died, and rose again from the dead, and so brought us again to our paternal home, whence we were driven. Thirdly, that we may remember our habitation is not of this world, but that we are here only as strangers and pilgrims; and that there is another and everlasting life prepared for us.

· 324 ·

The very name, the church, is the highest argument and proof of all hypocrites. The Pharisees, the scribes, yea, the whole senate of Jerusalem, cried out against Stephen, and said: "This man ceaseth not to speak blasphemous words against this holy place and the law." Cain, Ishmael, Saul, the Turks and Jews, bore and do bear the name and title of the church. But Moses finely solves this argument: "They have moved me to jealousy with that which is not God, they have provoked me to anger with their vanities: and I will move them to jealousy with those which are not a people: I will provoke them to anger with a foolish nation." Here was *quid pro quo;* as if God should say: "Could ye find in your hearts to forsake me? so can I again forsake you;" for God and nation, the Word and the church, are *correlativa;* the one cannot be without the other.

· 325 ·

Like as a child in the mother's womb is compassed about with a thin and tender caul, which the Greeks name *chorion* (the after-birth), and needs no more sustenance than so much as the *cotylidones,* from which the fruit receives nourishment, bring with them; nor does the after-birth break, except the fruit be ripe, and about to be timely brought to the light of this world; even so the church also is inclosed in the word and bound therein, and seeks none other doctrine concerning God's will than that which is revealed in the same; therewith she is content, and thereupon she remains and depends by faith, until she shall behold God's presence, and shall hear God himself preach of the mysteries and hidden things which on earth we see by faith.

But in case some vain-glorious professors, by un-

timely motion, force and break the after-birth, as
the papists and other seducers do in contemning the
office of preaching, and expect visions and revelations from heaven, this must be compared with un-
timely births, still-born children, and abortions.

· 326 ·

An olive tree will live and bear fruit two hundred
years; 'tis an image of the church; oil symbolizes
the gentle love of the gospel, as wine emblems the
doctrine of the law. There is such a natural unity
and affinity between the vine and the olive tree, that
when the branch of a vine is grafted upon an olive
tree, it bears both grapes and olives. In like manner, when the church, which is God's Word, is
planted in people's hearts, then it teaches both the
law and the gospel, using both doctrines, and from
both bringing fruit. The chestnut tree, in that it
produces all the better fruit when it is soundly
beaten, shadows forth man submissive to the law,
whose actions are not agreeable to God, until he has
been tried by tribulation. The lemon tree, with its
fruit, figures Christ; the lemon tree has the prop-
erty of bearing fruit at all seasons; when its fruits
are ripe, they drop off, and are succeeded by a fresh
growth; and this fruit is a sure remedy against

poison. Jesus Christ, when his ministers and champions depart from earth, replaces them by others; his produce is ever growing, and it is a sure remedy against the poison of the devil.

· 327 ·

The papists rely upon this: the church cannot err; we are the church, *ergo*, we cannot err. To the *major*, I make this answer: true, the church cannot err in doctrine, but in works and actions she may easily err, yea, and often does err; and therefore she prays: "Forgive us our trespasses," &c. The *minor* I utterly deny. Therefore when they argue and say, What the church teaches uprightly and pure, is true, this we admit; but when they argue and say: what the church does is upright and true, this we deny.

· 328 ·

Many boast of their title to the church, whereas they know not the true church; the holy prophets much opposed the false church. The prophet Isaiah, in the beginning of his first chapter, describes two sorts of churches. The upright and true church is a very small heap and number, of little or no esteem, and lying under the cross. But the false church is pompous, boasting, and presuming; she flourishes, and is held in high repute, like Sodom, of which St. Paul complains, Romans viii. and ix. The true church consists in God's election and calling; she is powerful and strong in weakness.

ON PREACHERS
AND PREACHING

· 329 ·

SOME there are that rail at the servants of God, and say: What though the Word and sacraments be upright and the truth, as indeed they be, when God speaks of them; 'tis not therefore God's Word when a man talks thereof.

· 330 ·

Divinity consists in use and practice, not in speculation and meditation. Every one that deals in speculations, either in household affairs or temporal government, without practice, is lost and nothing worth. When a tradesman makes his account, how much profit he shall reap in the year, but puts nothing in practice, he trades in vain speculations, and finds afterwards that his reckoning comes far too short. And thus it goes also with speculating divines, as is seen to this day, and as I know by experience.

· 331 ·

No man should undertake anything, except he be called thereunto. Calling is two-fold; either divine, which is done by the highest power, which is of faith; or else it is a calling of love, which is done by one's equal, as when one is desired by one's friend to preach a sermon. Both vocations are necessary to secure the conscience.

· 332 ·

Young people must be brought up to learn the Holy Scriptures; when such of them as know they are designed for the ministry present themselves and offer their service, upon a parish falling void, they do not intrude themselves, but are as a maid who, being arrived at woman's estate, when one makes suit to marry her, may do it, with a good and safe conscience towards God and the world. To thrust out another is to intrude; but when in the church a place is void, and thou sayest: I will willingly supply it, if ye please to make use of me; then thou art received, it is a true vocation and calling. Such was the manner of Isaiah, who said: "Here I am; send me." He came of himself when he heard they stood in need of a preacher; and so it ought to be; we must look whether people have need of us or no, and then whether we be desired or called.

· 333 ·

To the poor is the gospel declared, for the rich regard it not. If the pope maintained us not with that he has got, though much against his will, we might even starve for want of food. The pope has swallowed stolen goods, and must spew them all up again, as Job says: he must give them to those to whom he wishes evil. Scarce the fiftieth part is applied to the profit of the church; the rest he throws away; we obtain but the fragments under the table. But we are assured of better wages after this life; and, truly, if our hope were not fixed there, we were of all people the most miserable.

· 334 ·

I would not have preachers torment their hearers,
and detain them with long and tedious preaching,
for the delight of hearing vanishes therewith, and
the preachers hurt themselves.

· 335 ·

God was at Moses six several times before he
could get him forward; at last, after many excuses,
he went, but unwillingly. If I had been Moses, I
would, with the aid of some lawyer, have framed a
bill of complaint against our Lord God, for break-
ing his promise; for he said to Moses: "I will be
with thee," but he performed not what he promised.
In like manner God comforts and encourages with
similar promises in the gospel, saying: "And ye
shall find rest for your souls." But, alas! we see and
find the contrary, by John the Baptist, by his dear-
est Son, our blessed Saviour Christ Jesus, by all the
saints and holy martyrs, and by all true Christians;
so that, according to the lawyers, our Lord God has
lost the cause. Christ spake unto me as he spake
to St. Paul: "Arise and preach, and I will be with
thee." I have read that as an example. It is, indeed,
an office exceeding dangerous to preach Christ; had
I known as much before as I know now, I should

never have been drawn thereunto, but, with Moses,
would have said: "Send whom thou wilt send."

· 336 ·

One asked me: Which is greater and better—to
strive against adversaries, or to admonish and lift
up the weak? I answered: Both are very good and
necessary; but the latter is somewhat preferable;
the weak, by striving against the adversaries, are
also edified and bettered—both are God's gifts. He
that teaches, attend his teaching; he that admonishes, attend his admonishing.

· 337 ·

Dr. Forsteim asked Luther whence the art proceeded of speaking so powerfully, that both God-
fearing and ungodly people were moved? He answered: it proceeds from the first commandment of
God: "I am the Lord thy God;" i.e., against the
ungodly I am a strong and jealous God, towards
the good and godly, a merciful God; I do well and
show mercy to them, &c. For he will have us preach
hell-fire to the proud and haughty, and paradise to
the godly, reprove the wicked, and comfort the
good, &c. The instruments and work-tools of God
are different, even as one knife cuts better than an-

other. The sermons of Dr. Cordatus and Dr. Cru-
ciger are taken more to heart than the preaching of
many others.

· 338 ·

The world can well endure all sorts of preachers
except us, whom they will not hear; in former times
they were forced, under Popedom, to hear the ungodly tyrants, and to carry those on their shoulders that plagued them in body and soul, in wealth
and honour. But us, who by God's command reprove them, they will not hear: therefore the world
must go to rack. We must vanish by reason of poverty, but the papists, by reason of punishment;
their goods are not of proof, and are rejected of
God.

· 339 ·

A good preacher should have these properties and
virtues; first, to teach systematically; secondly, he
should have a ready wit; thirdly, he should be elo-
quent; fourthly, he should have a good voice;
fifthly, a good memory; sixthly, he should know
when to make an end; seventhly, he should be sure
of his doctrine; eighthly, he should venture and en-

gage body and blood, wealth and honour, in the word; ninthly, he should suffer himself to be mocked and jeered of every one.

· 340 ·

The defects in a preacher are soon spied; let a preacher be endued with ten virtues, and but one fault, yet this one fault will eclipse and darken all his virtues and gifts, so evil is the world in these times. Dr. Justus Jonas has all the good virtues and qualities a man may have; yet merely because he hums and spits, the people cannot bear that good and honest man.

· 341 ·

Luther's wife said to him: Sir, I heard your cousin, John Palmer, preach this afternoon in the parish church, whom I understood better than Dr. Pomer, though the Doctor is held to be a very excellent preacher. Luther answered: John Palmer preaches as ye women use to talk; for what comes into your minds, ye speak. A preacher ought to remain by the text, and deliver that which he has before him, to the end people may well understand it. But a preacher that will speak everything that comes in his mind, is like a maid that goes to market, and meeting another maid, makes a stand, and they hold together a goose-market.

· 342 ·

An upright shepherd and minister must improve his flock by edification, and also resist and defend it; otherwise, if resisting be absent, the wolf devours the sheep, and the rather, where they be fat and well fed. Therefore St. Paul presses it home upon Titus, that a bishop by sound doctrine should be able both to exhort and to convince gainsayers; that is, to resist false doctrine. A preacher must be both soldier and shepherd. He must nourish, defend, and teach; he must have teeth in his mouth, and be able to bite and to fight.

There are many talking preachers, but there is nothing in them save only words; they can talk much, but teach nothing uprightly. The world has always had such Thrasos, such boasting throat-criers.

· 343 ·

I know of no greater gift than that we have, namely, harmony in doctrine, so that throughout the principalities and imperial cities of Germany, they teach in conformity with us. Though I had the gift to raise the dead, what were it, if all other preachers taught against me? I would not exchange this concord for the Turkish empire.

· 344 ·

God often lays upon the necks of haughty divines all manner of crosses and plagues to humble them; and therein they are well and rightly served; for they will have honour, whereas this only belongs to our Lord God. When we are found true in our vocations and calling, then we have reaped honour sufficient, though not in this life, yet in that to come; there we shall be crowned with the unchangeable crown of honour, "which is laid up for us." Here on earth we must seek for no honour, for it is written: Woe unto you when men shall bless you. We belong not to this life, but to another far better. The world loves that which is its own; we must content ourselves with that which it bestows upon us, scoffing, flouting, and contempt. I am sometimes glad that my scholars and friends are pleased to give me such wages; I desire neither honour nor crown here on earth, but I will have compensation from God, the just judge in heaven.

From the year of our Lord 1518, to the present

time, every Maunday Thursday, at Rome, I have
been by the pope excommunicated and cast into
hell; yet I still live. For every year, on Maunday
Thursday, all heretics are excommunicated at Rome,
among whom I am always put first and chief. This
do they on that blessed, sanctified day, whereas
they ought rather to render thanks to God for the
great benefit of his holy supper, and for his bitter
death and passion. This is the honour and crown
we must expect and have in this world. God sometimes can endure honour in lawyers and physicians;
but in divines he will no way suffer it; for a boasting and an ambitious preacher soon contemns
Christ, who with his blood has redeemed poor
sinners.

· 345 ·

A preacher should need know how to make a
right difference between sinners, between the impenitent and confident, and the sorrowful and penitent; otherwise the whole Scripture is locked up.
When Amsdorf began to preach before the princes
at Schmalcalden, with great earnestness he said:
The gospel belongs to the poor and sorrowful, and
not to you princes, great persons and courtiers that

live in continual joy and delight, in secureness, void
of all tribulation.

· 346 ·

A continual hatred is between the clergy and laity,
and not without cause; for the unbridled people,
citizens, gentry, nobility, yea, and great princes
also, refuse to be reproved. But the office of a
preacher is to reprove such sinners as lie in open
sin, and offend against both the first and second
table of God's commandments; yet reproof is grievous for them to hear, wherefore they look upon the
preachers with sharp eyes.

· 347 ·

To speak deliberately and slowly best becomes
a preacher; for thereby he may the more effectually
and impressively deliver his sermon. Seneca writes
of Cicero, that he spake deliberately from the heart.

· 348 ·

God in the Old Testament made the priests rich;
Annas and Caiaphas had great revenues. But the
ministers of the Word, in which is offered everlasting life and salvation by grace, are suffered to die

of hunger and poverty, yea, are driven and hunted away.

· 349 ·

We ought to direct ourselves in preaching according to the condition of the hearers, but most preachers commonly fail herein; they preach that which little edifies the poor simple people. To preach plain and simply is a great art: Christ himself talks of tilling ground, of mustard seed, &c.; he used altogether homely and simple similitudes.

· 350 ·

When a man first comes into the pulpit, he is much perplexed to see so many heads before him. When I stand there I look upon none, but imagine they are all blocks that are before me.

· 351 ·

I would not have preachers in their sermons use Hebrew, Greek, or foreign languages, for in the church we ought to speak as we use to do at home, the plain mother tongue, which every one is acquainted with. It may be allowed in courtiers, lawyers, advocates, &c., to use quaint, curious words. Doctor Staupitz is a very learned man, yet he is a very irksome preacher; and the people had rather hear a plain brother preach, that delivers his words simply to their understanding, than he. In churches no praising or extolling should be sought after. St. Paul never used such high and stately words as Demosthenes and Cicero did, but he spake, properly and plainly, words which signified and showed high and stately matters, and he did well.

· 352 ·

If I should write of the heavy burthen of a godly preacher, which he must carry and endure, as I know by mine own experience, I should scare every man from the office of preaching. But I assure myself that Christ at the last day will speak friendly unto me, though he speaks very unkindly now. I bear upon me the malice of the whole world, the hatred of the emperor, of the pope, and of all their retinue. Well, on in God's name; seeing I am come into the lists, I will fight it out. I know my quarrel and cause are upright and just.

· 353 ·

It is a great thing to be an upright minister and preacher; if our Lord God himself drove it not forward, there would but little good ensue. Preachers

must be endued with a great spirit, to serve people
in body and soul, in wealth and honour, and yet,
nevertheless, suffer and endure the greatest danger
and unthankfulness. Hence Christ said to Peter
thrice: "Peter, lovest thou me?" Afterwards he
said: "Feed my sheep;" as if to say: Peter, if thou
wilt be an upright shepherd, and careful of souls,
then thou must love me; otherwise, it is impossible
for thee to be an upright and a careful shepherd;
thy love to me must do the deed.

· 354 ·

Our manner of life is as evil as is that of the
papists. Wickliffe and Huss assailed the immoral
conduct of papists; but I chiefly oppose and resist
their doctrine; I affirm roundly and plainly, that
they preach not the truth. To this am I called; I
take the goose by the neck, and set the knife to its
throat. When I can show that the papist's doctrine
is false, which I have shown, then I can easily prove
that their manner of life is evil. For when the word
remains pure, the manner of life, though something
therein be amiss, will be pure also. The pope has
taken away the pure word and doctrine, and brought
in another word and doctrine, which he has hanged
upon the church. I shook all Popedom with this one

point, that I teach uprightly, and mix up nothing else. We must press the doctrine onwards, for that breaks the neck of the pope. Therefore the prophet Daniel rightly pictured the pope, that he would be a king that would do according to his own will, that is, would regard neither spirituality nor temporality, but say roundly: Thus and thus will I have it. For the pope derives his institution neither from divine nor from human right; but is a self-chosen human creature and intruder. Therefore the pope must needs confess, that he governs neither by divine nor human command. Daniel calls him a god, *Maosim;* he had almost spoken it plainly out, and said *Mass,* which word is written, Deut. xxvi. St. Paul read Daniel thoroughly, and uses nearly his words, where he says: The son of perdition will exalt himself above all that is called God, or that is worshipped, &c., 2 Thes. ii.

· 355 ·

The humility of hypocrites is, of all pride, the greatest and most haughty, as that of the Pharisee who humbled himself and gave God thanks, but soon spoiled all again, when he said: "I am not like others, &c., nor as this publican." There are people who flatter themselves, and think they only are wise; they contemn and deride the opinions of all others; they will allow of nothing but only what pleases them.

· 356 ·

Ambition is the rankest poison to the church, when it possesses preachers. It is a consuming fire. The Holy Scripture is given to destroy the desires of the flesh; therefore we must not therein seek after temporal honour. I much marvel for what cause people are proud and haughty; we are born in sin, and every moment in danger of death. Are we proud of our scabs and scalds? we, who are altogether an unclean thing.

· 357 ·

Honour might be sought for in Homer, Virgil, and in Terence, and not in the Holy Scripture; for Christ says: "Hallowed be thy name—not ours, but thine be the glory." Christ charges us to preach God's Word. We preachers should of the world be held and esteemed as *injusti stulti*, to the end God be *justus, sapiens, et misericors*; that is his title, which he will leave to none other. When we leave to God his name, his kingdom, and will, then will he also give unto us our daily bread, remit our sins, and deliver us from the devil and all evil. Only his honour he will have to himself.

· 358 ·

It were but reasonable I should in my old age have some rest and peace, but now those that should be with and for me, fall upon me. I have plague enough with my adversaries, therefore my brethren should not vex me. But who is able to resist? They are fresh, lusty, young people, and have lived in idleness; I am now aged, and have had much labour and pains. Nothing causes Osiander's pride more than his idle life; for he preaches but twice a week, yet has a yearly stipend of four hundred guilders.

· 359 ·

God in wonderful wise led us out of the darkness of the sophists, and cast me into the game, now more than twenty years since. It went weakly forward at the first, when I began to write against the gross error of indulgences. At that time Doctor Jerome withstood me, and said: What will you do, they will not endure it? but, said I, what if they must endure it?

Soon after him came Silvester Prierio into the list; he thundered and lightned against me with his syllogisms, saying: Whosoever makes doubt of any one sentence or act of the Romish church, is a heretic: Martin Luther doubts thereof; *ergo*, he is a heretic. Then it went on, for the pope makes a three-fold distinction of the church. First, a substantial, *i.e.*, the body of the church. Secondly, a significant church, *i.e.*, the cardinals. Thirdly, an operative and powerful church; *i.e.*, the pope himself. No mention is made of a council, for the pope will be the powerful church above the Holy Scripture and councils.

· 360 ·

Our auditors, for the most part are epicurean; they measure our preaching as they think good, and will have easy days.

The Pharisees and Sadducees were Christ's enemies, yet they heard him willingly; the Pharisees, to the end they might lay hold on him; the Sadducees, that they might flout and deride him. The Pharisees are our friars; the Sadducees, our gentry, citizens, and country folk: our gentlemen give us the hearing, and believe us, yet will do what seems good to them; that is, they remain epicureans.

· 361 ·

A preacher should be a logician and a rhetorician, that is, he must be able to teach, and to admonish; when he preaches touching an article, he must, first, distinguish it. Secondly, he must define, describe, and show what it is. Thirdly, he must produce sentences out of the Scriptures, therewith to prove and strengthen it. Fourthly, he must, with examples, explain and declare it. Fifthly, he must adorn it with similitudes; and, lastly, he must admonish and rouse up the lazy, earnestly reprove all the disobedient, all false doctrine, and the authors thereof; yet, not out of malice and envy, but only to God's honour, and the profit and saving health of the people.

· 362 ·

Scripture requires humble hearts, that hold God's Word in honour, love, and worth, and that pray continually: "Lord, teach me thy ways and statutes." But the Holy Ghost resists the proud, and will not dwell with them. And although some for a time diligently study in Holy Scripture and teach and preach Christ uprightly, yet, as soon as they become proud, God excludes them out of the church. There-

fore, every proud spirit is a heretic, not in act and
deed, yet before God.

But it is a hard matter for one who has some
particular gift and quality above another, not to
be haughty, proud, and presumptuous, and not to
contemn others; therefore God suffers them that
have great gifts to fall many times into heavy tribulations, to the end they may learn, when God draws
away his hand, that then they are of no value. St.
Paul was constrained to bear on his body the sting
or thorn of the flesh, to preserve him from haughti-
ness. And if Philip Melancthon were not now and
then plagued in such sort as he is, he would have
strange conceits.

· 363 ·

I learn by preaching to know what the world, the
flesh, the malice and wickedness of the devil is, all
which could not be known before the gospel was
revealed and preached, for up to that time I thought
there were no sins but incontinence and lechery.

· 364 ·

At court these rules ought to be observed: we
must cry aloud, and accuse; for neither the gospel

nor modesty belong to the court; we must be harsh, and set our faces as flints; we must, instead of Christ, who is mild and friendly, place Moses with his horns in the court. Therefore I advise my chaplains and ministers to complain at court of their wants, miseries, poverty, and necessities; for I myself preached concerning the same before the prince elector, who is both good and godly, but his courtiers do what they please. Philip Melancthon and Justus Jonas were lately called in question at court, for the world's sake; but they made this answer: Luther is old enough, and knows how and what to preach.

· 365 ·

Cursed are all preachers that in the church aim at high and hard things, and, neglecting the saving health of the poor unlearned people, seek their own honour and praise, and therewith to please one or two ambitious persons.

When I preach, I sink myself deep down. I regard neither Doctors nor Magistrates, of whom are here in this church above forty; but I have an eye to the multitude of young people, children, and servants, of whom are more than two thousand. I preach to those, directing myself to them that have need thereof. Will not the rest hear me? The door stands open unto them; they may begone. I see that the ambition of preachers grows and increases; this will do the utmost mischief in the church, and produce great disquietness and discord; for they will needs teach high things touching matters of state, thereby aiming at praise and honour; they will please the worldly wise, and meantime neglect the simple and common multitude.

An upright, godly, and true preacher should direct his preaching to the poor, simple sort of people, like a mother that stills her child, dandles and plays with it, presenting it with milk from her own breast, and needing neither malmsey nor muscadin for it. In such sort should also preachers carry themselves, teaching and preaching plainly, that the simple and unlearned may conceive and comprehend, and retain what they say. When they come to me, to Melancthon, to Dr. Pomer, &c., let them show their cunning, how learned they be; they shall be well put to their trumps. But to sprinkle out Hebrew, Greek, and Latin in their public sermons, savours merely of show, according with neither time nor place.

· 366 ·

In the Psalm it is said: Their voice went out into
the whole world. But St. Paul to the Romans gives
it thus: "Their sound went out into all the earth,"
which is all one. Many sentences are in the Bible,
wherein St. Paul observed the translation of the
Seventy Interpreters, for he contemned them not;
and whereas he was preacher to the Greeks, therefore he was constrained to preach as they understood.

In such sort did he use that sentence, 1 Cor. xv.:
"Death is swallowed up in victory," whereas in the
Hebrew, it is "in the end;" yet 'tis all one. St. Paul
was very rich and flowing in words; one of his
words contains three of Cicero's orations, or the
whole of Isaiah and Jeremiah. O! he was an excellent preacher; he is not in vain named *vas electum*.
Our Lord God said: I will give a preacher to the
world that shall be precious. There was never any
that understood the Old Testament so well as St.
Paul, except John the Baptist, and John the Divine.
St. Peter excels also. St. Matthew and the rest well
describe the histories, which are very necessary; but
as to the things and words of the Old Testament,
they never mention what is couched therein.

St. Paul translated much out of Hebrew into Greek, which none besides were able to do; in handling one chapter, he often expounds four, five, or six. Oh, he dearly loved Moses and Isaiah, for they, together with king David, were the chief prophets. The words and things of St. Paul are taken out of Moses and the Prophets.

Young divines ought to study Hebrew, to the end they may be able to compare Greek and Hebrew words together, and discern their properties, natures, and strength.

OF THE FATHERS OF THE CHURCH

· 367 ·

I WILL not presume to criticise too closely the writings of the Fathers, seeing they are received of the church, and have great applause, for then I should be held an apostate; but whoso reads Chrysostom, will find he digresses from the chief points, and proceeds to other matters, saying nothing, or very little, of that which pertains to the business. When I was expounding the Epistle to the Hebrews, and turned to what Chrysostom had written thereupon, I found nothing to the purpose; yet I believe that he at that time, as being the chief rhetorician, had many hearers, though he taught without profit; for the chief office of a preacher is to teach uprightly, and diligently to look to the chief points and grounds whereon he stands, and so instruct and teach the hearers, that they understand aright, and may be able to say: this is well taught. When this is done, he may avail himself of rhetoric to adorn his subject and admonish the people.

· 368 ·

Epiphanius compiled a history of the church long before Jerome; his writings are good and profitable, and, if separated from dissentious arguments, worth printing.

· 369 ·

I much like the hymns and spiritual songs of Prudentius; he was the best of the Christian poets; if he had lived in the time of Virgil, he would have been extolled above Horace. I wish the verses of

Prudentius were read in schools, but schools are now become heathenish, and the Holy Scripture is banished from them, and sophisticated through philosophy.

· 370 ·

We must read the Fathers cautiously, and lay them in the gold balance, for they often stumbled and went astray, and mingled in their books many monkish things. Augustin had more work and labour to wind himself out of the Fathers' writings, than he had with the heretics. Gregory expounds the five pounds mentioned in the gospel, which the husbandman gave to his servants to put to use, to be the five senses, which the beasts also possess. The two pounds, he construes to be the reason and understanding.

· 371 ·

The more I read the books of the Fathers, the more I find myself offended; for they were but men, and, to speak the truth, with all their repute and authority, undervalued the books and writings of the sacred apostles of Christ. The papists were not ashamed to say, What is the Scripture? we must read the holy fathers and teachers, for they drew and sucked the honey out of the Scripture. As if God's Word were to be understood and conceived by none but by themselves, whereas the heavenly Father says: "Him shall ye hear," who in the gospel taught most plainly in parables and similitudes.

· 372 ·

Augustin was the ablest and purest of all the doctors, but he could not of himself bring back things to their original condition, and he often complains that the bishops, with their traditions and ordinances, troubled the church more than did the Jews with their laws.

· 373 ·

Faithful Christians should heed only the embassy of our blessed Saviour Christ, and what he says. All they who alter and construe the gospel through human authority, power and repute, act very unchristianlike and against God. No temporal potentate allows his ambassador to exceed his instructions, not in one word; yet we, in this celestial and divine embassage and legation, will be so presumptuous as to add and diminish to and from our heavenly instructions, according to our own vain conceits and self-will.

· 374 ·

I am persuaded that if at this time, St. Peter, in person, should preach all the articles of Holy Scripture, and only deny the pope's authority, power, and primacy, and say, that the pope is not the head of all Christendom, they would cause him to be hanged. Yea, if Christ himself were again on earth, and should preach, without all doubt the pope would crucify him again. Therefore let us expect the same treatment; but better is it to build upon Christ, than upon the pope. If, from my heart, I did not believe that after this life there were another, then I would sing another song, and lay the burthen on another's neck.

· 375 ·

Lyra's Commentaries upon the Bible are worthy of all praise. I will order them diligently to be read, for they are exceeding good, especially on the historical part of the Old Testament. Lyra is very profitable to him that is well versed in the New Testament. The commentaries of Paulus and Simigerus are very cold; they may well be omitted and left out, if Lyra should be reprinted.

· 376 ·

Jerome should not be numbered among the teachers of the church, for he was a heretic; yet I believe that he is saved through faith in Christ. He speaks not of Christ, but merely carries his name in his mouth.

· 377 ·

The master of sentences, Peter Lombard, was a very diligent man, and of a high understanding; he wrote many excellent things. If he had wholly given himself to the Holy Scriptures, he had been indeed a great and a leading doctor of the church: but he introduced into his books unprofitable questions, sophisticating and mingling all together. The school divines were fine and delicate wits, but they lived not in such times as we. They got so far that they taught mankind were not complete, pure, or sound, but wounded in part, yet they said people by their own power, without grace, could fulfil the law; though when they had obtained grace, they were able more easily to accomplish the law, of their own proper power.

Such and the like horrible things they taught; but they neither saw nor felt Adam's fall, nor that the law of God is a spiritual law, requiring a complete and full obedience inwardly and outwardly, both in body and soul.

· 378 ·

Gabriel Biel wrote a book upon the canon in the mass, which at that time I held for the best; my heart bled when I read it. I still keep those books which tormented me. Scotus wrote very well upon the *Magister sententiarum*, and diligently essayed to teach upon those matters. Occam was an able and sensible man.

OF THE PATRI-ARCHS AND PROPHETS

· 379 ·

DAVID'S fall was very offensive, for the holy man fell into adultery, murder, and despising of God.

He was afterwards visited and punished by God in such sort, that the whole nation forsook him. His counsellors—yea, his best beloved son, conspired and made a league against him, who before had such high fortune, and was held in such esteem.

On account of these offences, the ungodly, doubtless, boasted, and said: "Where is the king now? where is now his God? what has become of his good fortune and prosperity?" For no doubt there were many kings more powerful than David; as the king of the Moabites, whom Isaiah calls a three-yeared cow; that is, strong, powerful, and fat.

It has always been so in the world—that it has gone evil with the godly, and well with the ungodly; of this complaint is made in many Psalms. We see at this day, that the popish bishops and ungodly princes live in great honour, wealth, and power, while good and God-fearing people are in poverty, disgrace, and trouble.

The Greek tragedies are not to be compared with the history of David.

· 380 ·

All kings, princes, rulers, and ministers, sin of necessity, and therefore have special need of the

remission of sins. I am persuaded that Ahab was
saved, inasmuch as God said to the prophet: "Seest
thou not how Ahab boweth himself before me?"
For to whom God affords speech, that is, his word
and promise, with him it stands well. Therefore,
doubtless, he was saved, notwithstanding the Scriptures witness against him, even to his death. He
believed the promise of the Messiah, and so at his
death got hold of the forgiveness of sins. In like
manner I am persuaded also of all those of whom
the Scripture says: "And he slept with his fathers,"
that they are all in heaven. For this word, slept,
shows some good in the Scriptures. But of whom it
is written: They were made away and slain by the
enemies, or were devoured and torn in pieces by
wild beasts, I am persuaded they are lost and
damned.

· 381 ·

Although God charged David to build the temple,
he could not perform it, because he had shed much
blood, and had carried the sword; not that he did
wrong therein, but that he could not be the figure
or type of Christ, who must have a peaceable kingdom, without shedding of blood. But Solomon was

to accomplish it, who is called peaceable, through which Christ's kingdom was signified.

· 382 ·

It is with us, as it was in the time of Judas Maccabæus, who defended his people, and yet was not able to suppress the enemies who possessed the government; while his own people were unthankful, and wrought him great mischief; these two oppressions make one weary.

The legends of the patriarchs far excelled the holiness of all the saints; for they went on in simple obedience towards God, in the works of their vocation. They performed such things as came to their hand, according to God's command, without respect; therefore Sara, Abraham's wife, excels all other women.

· 383 ·

Philip Melancthon demanded of Luther: how it was, that though David was instituted and ordained a king immediately of God, yet he had many tribulations and plagues, as his psalms show? Luther said: David was not acquainted with many good days; he was plagued by the ungodly and false teachers, he saw that his people banded against him, he endured and suffered many insurrections and tumults, which taught him his lesson to pray. When he was without tribulation, he grew giddy-headed and secure, as we see in his adultery, and his murder of Uriah.

Ah, Lord God! how is it thou sufferest such great people to fall? This David had six wives, who doubtless were wise and understanding women; as was the wise Abigail; if they were all such, he was furnished with surpassing wives. Moreover, he had ten concubines; yet, notwithstanding, he was an adulterer.

· 384 ·

Job had many tribulations; he was also plagued of his own friends, who fiercely assaulted him. The text says, that his friends fell upon him, and were full of wrath against him; they tormented him thoroughly, but he held his peace, suffered them to talk their talk, as if he should say, you know not what you prate about. Job is an example of God's goodness and mercy; for how upright and holy soever he was, yet he sorely fell into temptation; but he was not forsaken, he was again delivered and redeemed through God's grace and mercy.

· 385 ·

Melancthon discoursing with Luther touching the prophets, who continually boast thus: "Thus saith the Lord," asked whether God in person spoke with them or no. Luther replied: They were very holy, spiritual people, who seriously contemplated upon holy and divine things; therefore God spake with them in their consciences, which the prophets held as sure and certain revelations.

We read in the books of the Jews that Isaiah was slain by king Ahaz, because he said: "I saw the Lord sitting upon a throne," &c. Doubtless, Ahaz said unto him: Thou wretch! how darest thou presume to say, "Thou hast seen the Lord?" whereas God said to Moses, "Shall a man see me, and live?" Thou art an insane heretic; thou blasphemest God; thou art worthy of death; take him away. And many think it quite just that Isaiah was slain for this, not enduring that any man should say he had done or seen greater things than Moses.

· 386 ·

The history of Elijah is awful, and almost incredible. It was a fierce anger indeed, that so holy a man should pray it might not rain; but he saw that the teachers were slain, and that good and God-fearing people were hunted down, and persecuted. Therefore he prayed against those upon whom, with words and preaching, he could not prevail.

· 387 ·

The majesty of the prophet Jonah is surpassing. He has but four chapters, and yet he moved therewith the whole kingdom, so that in his weakness, he was justly a figure and a sign of the Lord Christ. Indeed, it is surprising, that Christ should recur to this but in four words. Moses likewise, in few words describes the creation, the history of Abraham, and other great mysteries; but he spends much time in describing the tent, the external sacrifices, the kidneys and so on; the reason is, he saw that the world greatly esteemed outward things, which they beheld with their carnal eyes, but that which was spiritual, they soon forgot.

The history of the prophet Jonah is almost incredible, sounding more strange than any poet's fable; if it were not in the Bible, I should take it for a lie; for consider, how for the space of three days he was in the great belly of the whale, whereas in three hours he might have been digested and changed into the nature, flesh and blood of that monster; may not this be said, to live in the midst of death? In comparison of this miracle, the wonderful passage through the Red Sea was nothing.

But what appears more strange is, that after he was delivered, he began to be angry, and to expostulate with the gracious God, touching a small matter not worth a straw. It is a great mystery. I am ashamed of my exposition upon this prophet, in that I so weakly touch the main point of this wonderful miracle.

· 388 ·

The harsh and sharp words of the prophets go to the heart, yet when they say: "Jerusalem shall fall, and be destroyed," the Jews held such preaching merely heretical, and would not endure it.

Even so say I: the Romish church shall fall, and be destroyed; but the papists will neither believe nor endure it; it is impossible, say they, for it is written in the article: "I believe in the holy Christian church." Many kings were destroyed before Jerusalem, as Sennacherib, &c.; when the prophet Jeremiah said: "Jerusalem shall be destroyed," which he spake through the Holy Ghost, so it fell out.

If the pope could bring against me only one such argument as the Jews had against Jeremiah and other prophets, it were not possible for me to subsist. But the pope disputes with me, not according to justice and equity, but with the sword and his power. He uses no written law, but club law. If I had no other argument against the pope than *de facto*, I would instantly hang myself; but my dispute is *jus*.

· 389 ·

An upright Christian is like unto Jonah, who was cast into the sea, that is, into hell. He beheld the mouth of the monster gaping to devour him, and lay three days in its dark belly, without consuming. This history should be unto us one of the greatest comforts, and a manifest sign of the resurrection from the dead.

In such sort does God humble those that are his. But afterwards, Jonah went too far; he presumed to command God Almighty, and became a great man-slayer and a murderer, for he desired that a great city and many people should be utterly destroyed, though God chose to spare them. This was a strange saint.

· 390 ·

To translate the prophets well from the Hebrew

tongue, is a precious, great, and glorious work;
no man before me well attained thereunto, and to
me it is a hard task; let me be once clear from it,
it shall rest.

· 391 ·

It is easy to be conceived, that David dealt uprightly, and repentingly, in not rejecting Bathsheba,
Uriah's wife, but marrying her. Forasmuch as he
had shamed her, it was fitting for him to restore
her to honour. God was also pleased with that con-
junction; yet, for a punishment of the adultery, God
caused the son, begotten in it, soon to die.

· 392 ·

No man, since the apostles' time, has rightly understood the legend of Abraham. The apostles themselves did not sufficiently extol or explain Abraham's
faith, according to its worth and greatness. I much
marvel that Moses so slightly remembers him.

Job at one time lost ten children and all his
cattle; he was punished in body and in goods, yet
it was nothing in comparison of David's troubles,
for though David had the promise which could
neither fail nor deceive—namely, where God says:
"Thou shalt be king," God thoroughly powdered

and peppered his kingdom for his tooth; no miserable man ever surpassed David.

· 393 ·

The reason that Abraham gave to Agar, his concubine, and Ishmael, his son, only one flagon of wine, was that she might know she had no right to demand anything of the inheritance, but that what was given her proceeded out of good will, not of any obligation or reason of law, yet that, neverless, she might repair again to Abraham, and fetch more.

The text in Genesis says: "Isaac and Ishmael buried Abraham;" hence it appears that Ishmael was not always with his father, but was nurtured out of the father's goodness and bounty, which was done to this end, that Abraham, intending to lead Christ through the right line, therefore Ishmael was separated like Esau.

· 394 ·

I hold that Jacob was a poor, perplexed man; I would willingly, if I could, frame a Laban out of the rich glutton in the gospel of Luke, and a Jacob out of Lazarus who lay before the gate. I am glad that Rachael sat upon the idols, thereby to spite her father Laban.

· 395 ·

Neither Cicero, nor Virgil, nor Demosthenes, are to be compared with David, in point of eloquence, as we see in the 119th Psalm, which he divides into two and twenty parts, each composed of eight verses, and yet all having but one thought—thy law is good. He had great gifts, and was highly favoured of God. I hold that God suffered him to fall so horribly, lest he should become too haughty and proud.

· 396 ·

Some are of opinion that David acted not well in that, upon his death-bed, he commanded Solomon his son to punish Shimei, who had cursed and thrown dirt at him, in his flight before Absalom. But I say he did well, for the office of a magistrate is to punish the guilty, and wicked malefactors. He had made a vow, indeed, not to punish him, but that was to hold only so long as he lived.

In so strange and confused a government, where no man knew who was cook or who butler, as we used to say, David was often constrained to look through the fingers at many abuses and wrongs. But afterwards, when in Solomon's time, there was peace, then through Solomon he punished. In tumultuous governments, a ruler dares not proceed as in time of peace, yet, at last, it is fitting that evil be punished; and as David says: *Maledixit mihi maledictionem malam.*

· 397 ·

Hezekiah was a very good and pious king, full of faith, yet he fell. God cannot endure that a human creature should trust and depend upon his own works. No man can enter into heaven, without the remission of sins.

· 398 ·

Elisha dealt uprightly, in permitting the children to be torn in pieces by two bears, for calling him bald-pate, since they mocked not him, but his God. And so as to the jeering and mocking of Elijah: "Thou man of God," &c., 'twas just that fire came down from heaven and devoured the mockers.

· 399 ·

Many strange things, according to human sense and reason, are written in the books of the kings; they seem to be slight and simple books, but in the spirit they are of great weight. David endured much; Saul persecuted and plagued him ten whole years; yet David remained constant in faith, and believed that the kingdom pertained unto him. I should have gone my way, and said: Lord! thou hast deceived me; wilt thou make me a king, and sufferest me in this sort to be tormented, persecuted, and plagued? But David was like a strong wall. He was also a good and a godly man; he refused to lay hands on the king when he had fit opportunity; for he had God's word, and that made him remain so steadfast; he was sure that God's word and promise never would or could fail him.

Surely Jonathan was an honest man, whom David loved entirely; he marked well that the kingdom belonged to David, therefore he intreated David not to root out him and his. Jonathan also wrought wonders, when he, alone with his armour-bearer, went over the mountain, and slew and destroyed the Philistines; for, doubtless, he said in himself, the Lord that overcomes with many, is able also to overcome with few. His death was a great grief to

David. So it often happens, that the good are punished for the sake of the wicked and ungodly. The Son of God himself was not spared.

OF THE APOSTLES
AND DISCIPLES
OF CHRIST

· 400 ·

THE reason why the disciples were afraid when Christ came unto them, the doors being shut, was, that they saw how it lately went with their Lord and Master, and feared it might go even so with them, especially considering that at the same time the Jews intended to act with violence against them. For as yet they scarcely believed that Christ was risen again from the dead, as may be gathered from the two disciples going to Emmaus, who said: We hoped he should have redeemed Israel; as much as to say: Now all our hope is at an end.

· 401 ·

The reason why the papists boast more of St. Peter than of St. Paul is this: St. Paul had the sword, St. Peter the keys, and they esteem more of the keys, to open the coffers, to filch and steal, and to fill their thievish purse, than of the sword. That Caiaphas, Pilate, and St. Peter came to Rome, and appeared before the emperor, is mere fable; the histories touching that point do not accord. Christ died in the reign of Tiberius Cæsar, who governed five years after his death. All histories unanimously agree, that St. Peter and St. Paul died under the emperor Nero, whose last year was the five and twentieth year after the death of Christ. But St. Peter was eighteen years at Jerusalem after Christ's death, as the Epistle to the Galatians witnesses; and after that, he was seven years at Antioch. Then, as they fable, he ruled afterwards five-and-twenty years at Rome.

No pope among them all yet ruled five-and-twenty years; and, according to this reckoning, St. Peter was not crucified under Nero. Saint Luke writes, that St. Paul was two whole years at liberty in Rome, and went abroad; he mentions nothing at all of St. Peter. It is a thing not to be believed that St. Peter ever was at Rome.

· 402 ·

Saint John the Evangelist wrote, at first, touching the true nature of faith—that our salvation depends only upon Christ the Son of God and Mary, who purchased it with his bitter passion and death, and through the word is received into the heart by faith, out of his mere mercy and grace. At last he was constrained to write in his epistle also of works, by reason of the wickedness of those that, void of all shame, abused the gospel through indulging the flesh.

OF ANGELS

· 403 ·

AN angel is a spiritual creature created by God without a body, for the service of Christendom and of the church.

· 404 ·

The acknowledgment of angels is needful in the church. Therefore godly preachers should teach them logically. First, they should show what angels are, namely, spiritual creatures without bodies. Secondly, what manner of spirits they are, namely, good spirits and not evil; and here evil spirits must also be spoken of, not created evil by God, but made so by their rebellion against God, and their consequent fall; this hatred began in Paradise, and will continue and remain against Christ and his church to the world's end. Thirdly, they must speak touching their function, which, as the epistle to the Hebrews (chap. i. v. 14) shows, is to present a mirror of humility to godly Christians, in that such pure and perfect creatures as the angels do minister unto us, poor and wretched people, in household and temporal policy, and in religion. They are our true and trusty servants, performing offices and works that one poor miserable mendicant would be ashamed to do for another. In this sort ought we to teach with care, method, and attention, touching the sweet and loving angels. Whoso speaks of them not in the order prescribed by logic, may speak of many irrelevant things, but little or nothing to edification.

· 405 ·

The angels are near to us, to those creatures

whom by God's command they are to preserve, to
the end we receive no hurt of the devil, though,
withal, they behold God's face, and stand before
him. Therefore when the devil intends to hurt us,
then the loving holy angels resist and drive him
away; for the angels have long arms, and although
they stand before the face and in the presence of
God and his son Christ, yet they are hard by and
about us in those affairs, which by God we are
commanded to take in hand. The devil is also near
and about us, incessantly tracking our steps, in
order to deprive us of our lives, our saving health,
and salvation. But the holy angels defend us from
him, insomuch that he is not able to work us such
mischief as willingly he would.

· 406 ·

It were not good for us to know how earnestly
the holy angels strive for us against the devil, or
how hard a combat it is. If we could see for how
many angels one devil makes work, we should be in
despair. Therefore the Holy Scriptures refers to
them in few words: "He hath given his angels
charge over thee," &c. Also: "The angel of the
Lord encampeth round about those that fear him,"
&c. Now, whosoever thou art, that fearest the Lord,

be of good courage, take thou no care, neither be faint-hearted, nor make any doubt of the angels' watching and protection; for most certainly they are about thee, and carry thee upon their hands. How or in what manner it is done, take thou no heed. God says it, therefore it is most sure and certain.

• 407 •

I believe that the angels are all up in arms, are putting on their harness, and girding their swords about them. For the last judgment draws nigh, and the angels prepare themselves for the combat, and to strike down Turk and pope into the bottomless pit.

OF TEMPTATION AND TRIBULATION

• 408 •

ALL heaviness of mind and melancholy come of the devil; especially these thoughts, that God is not gracious unto him: that God will have no mercy upon him, &c. Whosoever thou art, possessed with such heavy thoughts, know for certain, that they are a work of the devil. God sent his Son into the world, not to affright, but to comfort.

Therefore be of good courage, and think, that henceforward thou art not the child of a human creature, but of God, through faith in Christ, in whose name thou art baptized; therefore the spear of death cannot enter into thee; he has no right unto thee, much less can he hurt or prejudice thee, for he is everlastingly swallowed up through Christ.

· 409 ·

It is better for a Christian to be sorrowful than secure, as the people of the world are. Well is it for him that stands always in fear, yet knows he has in heaven a gracious God, for Christ's sake; as the Psalm says: "The Lord's delight is in them that fear him, and put their trust in his mercy."

There are two sorts of tribulations; one, of the spirit; another, of the flesh. Satan torments the conscience with lies, perverting that which is done uprightly, and according to God's Word; but the body, or flesh, he plagues in another kind.

No man ought to lay a cross upon himself, or to

adopt tribulation, as is done in Popedom; but if a cross or tribulation come upon him, then let him suffer it patiently, and know that it is good and profitable for him.

· 410 ·

Christ said to the adulteress: "Neither do I condemn thee, go, and sin no more." To the murderer, he said: "This day shalt thou be with me in Paradise." But to the Scribes and Pharisees, who set themselves against the righteousness of the gospel, Christ said: "Woe be unto you."

When one out of weakness denies God's Word, as many at this time do, under prince George, it is no sin against the Holy Ghost. Peter sinned in denying Christ, but not against the Holy Ghost. On the contrary, Judas persisted in sinning; he repented not aright, but remained hardened.

· 411 ·

It is impossible for a human heart, without crosses and tribulations, to think upon God.

· 412 ·

Not all can bear tribulations alike; some are bet-

ter able to bear a blow of the devil; as we three,
Philip Melancthon, John Calvin, and myself.

· 413 ·

David, doubtless, had worse devils than we, for
without great tribulations, he could not have had
so great and glorious revelations. David made
psalms: we also will make psalms, and sing as
well as we can, to the honour of our Lord God,
and to spite and mock the devil and his spouse.

· 414 ·

When David sang his song: "O my son Absalom,
my son, my son Absalom, would God I had died for
thee, O Absalom my son, my son," &c. Ah! how
sorrowful and perplexed a man was he. The very
words denote that his grief of heart was excessive.

The good and holy king had vehement tribulations and crosses, which altogether eclipsed and
darkened the promises made by God unto him. They
were fearful and horrible examples. To hold fast
and sure to the Word, in time of such trials and
vexations, as David did, Oh! this is of inestimable
value.

· 415 ·

The upright and true Christian church has to
strive not only with flesh and blood, but with spiritual wickedness in high places. The spiritual combat is most heavy and dangerous; flesh and blood
take away but only body, wife and children, house,
land, and what is temporal; but the spiritual evil
takes away the soul, everlasting life and salvation.

· 416 ·

The Lord our God is a God of humble and perplexed hearts, who are in need, tribulation, and
danger. If we were strong, we should be proud and
haughty. God shows his power in our weakness; he
will not quench the glimmering flax, neither will he
break in pieces the bruised reed.

· 417 ·

Faith's tribulation is the greatest and sharpest
torment, for faith must overcome all other tribulations; so that if faith be foiled, all other tribulations
must needs fall upon human creatures; but if faith
hold up her head, and be sound and in health, all
other tribulations and vexations must grow sick,

weak, and decrease. This tribulation of faith was
that thorn which St. Paul felt, and which pierced
through flesh and spirit, through soul and body.
Such tribulations was David possessed with, when
he made this psalm: "Lord, rebuke me not in thy
anger." No doubt he would rather have been slain
with a sword, than have suffered such wrath and
indignation from God.

· 418 ·

Heavy thoughts bring on physical maladies; when
the soul is oppressed, so is the body. Augustin said
well: *Anima plus est ubi amat, quàm ubi animat.*
When cares, heavy cogitations, sorrows, and passions superabound, they weaken the body, which,
without the soul, is dead, or like a horse without a
driver. But when the heart is at rest, and quiet, then
it takes care of the body, and gives it what pertains
thereunto. Therefore we ought to abandon and resist
anxious thoughts, by all possible means.

· 419 ·

The life of no human creature is without discon-
tent; every one has his tribulations, and many a
one, rather than be without them, will procure dis-

quietness to himself. No man is content with that which God gives him.

· 420 ·

Ah! how willingly would I now die, for I am faint and overwrought, and at this time I have a joyful and peaceable heart and conscience. I know full well, so soon as I shall be again in health, I neither shall have peace nor rest, but sorrow, weariness, and tribulations. But even that great man, St. Paul, could not be exempt from tribulations.

· 421 ·

When spiritual tribulations approach, we say: cursed be the day wherein I was born; and we begin to sweat. In such tribulations was our blessed Saviour Christ, in the garden, when he said: "Father, let this cup pass from me." Here the will was against the will, yet he turned himself presently according to his Father's will, and was comforted by an angel. Christ, who in our flesh was plagued and tempted, is the best mediator and advocate with God, in our tribulation. He is president, when we are only respondents, if we will but suffer him to mediate. Seems it God is angry with us when we are in tribulation and temptation, yet when we repent and believe, we shall find, that under such anger God's grace and goodness towards us lie hid. Therefore, let us patiently attend God's leisure, and constantly remain in hope.

· 422 ·

On the 8th of August, 1529, Luther, with his wife, lay sick of a fever. Overwhelmed with dysentery, sciatica, and a dozen other maladies, he said: God has touched me sorely, and I have been impatient: but God knows better than we whereto it serves. Our Lord God is like a printer, who sets the letters backwards, so that here we must so read them; when we are printed off, yonder, in the life to come, we shall read all clear and straightforward. Meantime we must have patience.

Tribulation is a right school and exercise of flesh and blood. The Psalms, almost in every verse, speak of nothing but tribulations, perplexities, sorrows, and troubles; they are a book of tribulations.

· 423 ·

Christ received the thief on the cross, and Paul, after so many blasphemings and prosecutions. We, then, have no cause at all to doubt. And, indeed, we

must all in that way attain to salvation. Yet, though
we have no cause to fear God's wrath, for old
Adam's sake we must stand in fear; for we cannot
take such hold on the grace and mercy of God as
we ought. He had but only the first six words in the
creed: "I believe in God the Father," yet these
were far above his natural wisdom, reason, and understanding.

· 424 ·

The devil plagues and torments us in the place
where we are most tender and weak. In Paradise, he
fell not upon Adam, but upon Eve. It commonly
rains where it was wet enough before.

When one is possessed with the doubt, that though
he call upon the Lord he cannot be heard, and that
God has turned his heart from him, and is angry,
cogitations which we suffer, which are forced upon
us, he must against them arm himself with God's
Word, promising to hear him. As to the when and
how God will hear him, this is stark naught; place,
time, and person are accidental things; the substance
and essence is the promise.

· 425 ·

I have often need, in my tribulations, to talk even

with a child, in order to expel such thoughts as the
devil possesses me with; and this teaches me not to
boast, as if of myself I were able to help myself, and
to subsist without the strength of Christ. I need one,
at times, to help me, who, in his whole body, has not
so much divinity as I have in one finger.

· 426 ·

In this life are many different degrees of tribulations, as there are different persons. Had another
had the tribulations which I have suffered, he would
long since have died; while I could not have endured the buffetings which St. Paul did, nor St.
Paul the tribulations which Christ suffered. The
greatest and heaviest grief is, when one dies in the
twinkling of an eye. But hereof we ought not to dispute, but to refer the same to God's judgment.

· 427 ·

When I am assailed with heavy tribulations, I
rush out among my pigs, rather than remain alone
by myself. The human heart is like a millstone in a
mill; when you put wheat under it, it turns and
grinds and bruises the wheat to flour; if you put no
wheat, it still grinds on, but then 'tis itself it grinds
and wears away. So the human heart, unless it be

occupied with some employment, leaves space for the devil, who wriggles himself in, and brings with him a whole host of evil thoughts, temptations, and tribulations, which grind out the heart.

· 428 ·

No papist among them will throw himself into the flames for his doctrine, whereas our people readily encounter fire and death, following therein the example of the holy martyrs, St. Agnes, St. Agatha, St. Vincent, St. Lawrence, &c. We are sheep for the slaughter. Only the other day, they burned, at Paris, two nobles and two magistrates, victims in the cause of the gospel, the king himself (Francis I), setting fire to the faggots.

· 429 ·

My tribulations are more necessary for me than meat and drink; and all they that feel them ought to accustom themselves thereunto, and learn to bear them. If Satan had not so plagued and exercised me, I should not have been so great an enemy unto him, or have been able to do him such hurt. Tribulations keep us from pride, and therewith increase the acknowledgment of Christ and of God's gifts and benefits. For, from the time I began to be in tribulation, God gave me the victory of overcoming that confounded, cursed, and blasphemous life wherein I lived in Popedom. God did the business in such a way, that neither the emperor nor the pope was able to suppress me, but the devil must come and set upon me, to the end God's strength may be known in my weakness.

· 430 ·

Our tribulations and doubts, wherewith the devil plagues us, can be driven away by no better means than by contemning him; as when one contemns a fierce cur, in passing quietly by him, the dog then not only desists from biting, but also from barking; but when one enrages him by timorously throwing something at him, then he falls upon and bites him. Even so, when the devil sees that we fear him, he ceases not to torment and plague us.

· 431 ·

A woman at Eisenach lay very sick, having endured horrible paroxysms, which no physician was able to cure, for it was directly a work of the devil. She had had swoonings, and four paroxysms, each lasting three or four hours. Her hands and feet bent in the form of a horn; she was chill and cold; her tongue rough and dry; her body much swollen. She seeing Luther, who came to visit her, was much rejoiced thereat, raised herself up, and said: Ah! my loving father in Christ, I have a heavy burthen upon me, pray to God for me; and so fell down in her bed again. Whereupon Luther sighed, and said: "God rebuke thee, Satan, and command thee that thou suffer this, his divine creature, to be at peace." Then turning himself towards the standers by, he said: "She is plagued of the devil in the body, but the soul is safe, and shall be preserved; therefore let us give thanks to God, and pray for her;" and so they all prayed aloud the Lord's prayer. After which, Luther concluded with these words: "Lord God, heavenly Father! who hast commanded us to pray for the sick, we beseech thee, through Jesus Christ, thy only beloved Son, that thou wouldst deliver this thy servant from her sickness, and from the hands of the devil. Spare, O Lord, her soul, which, together with her body, thou hast purchased and redeemed from the power of sin, of death, and of the devil." Whereupon the sick woman said "Amen." The night following she took rest, and the next day was graciously delivered from her disease and sickness.

· 432 ·

When Satan will not leave off tempting thee, then
bear with patience, hold on hand and foot, nor faint,
as if there would be no end thereof, but stand
courageously, and attend God's leisure, knowing that
what the devil cannot accomplish by his sudden and
powerful assaults, he thinks to gain by craft, by
persevering to vex and tempt thee, thereby to make
thee faint and weary, as in the Psalm is noted:
"Many a time have they afflicted me from my youth
up; yet they have not prevailed against me," &c.
But be fully assured, that in this sport with the devil,
God, with all his holy angels, takes delight and joy;
and assure thyself, also, that the end thereof will be
blessed and happy, which thou shalt certainly find to
thy everlasting comfort.

· 433 ·

Concerning predestination, it is best to begin below, at Christ as then we both hear and find the
Father; for all those that have begun at the top have
broken their necks. I have been thoroughly plagued
and tormented with such cogitations of predestination; I would needs know how God intended to deal
with me, &c. But at last, God be praised! I clean
left them; I took hold again on God's revealed

word; higher I was not able to bring it, for a human
creature can never search out the celestial will of
God; this God hides, for the sake of the devil, to
the end the crafty spirit may be deceived and put
to confusion. The revealed will of God the devil has
learned from us, but God reserves his secret will to
himself. It is sufficient for us to learn and know
Christ in his humanity, in which the Father has revealed himself.

· 434 ·

Christ, on the tenth day, came again into Jerusalem, and on the fourteenth day he was killed. His
cogitations and tribulations then were concerning
the sins of the whole world, concerning God's wrath
and death, of which all ought to stand in fear. But
before he was thus personally made sin for us, he
was a man of sorrows, and acquainted with grief;
his tribulations were concerning his labour and
pains, which he knew would be spent in vain upon
his own nation, the Jews, and over which he wept
bitterly, because they knew not the time of their
visitation.

· 435 ·

More and greater sins are committed when people

are alone than when they are in society. When Eve, in paradise, walked by herself, the devil deceived her. In solitary places are committed murders, robberies, adulteries, &c.; for in solitude the devil has place and occasion to mislead people. But whosoever is in honest company is ashamed to sin, or at least has no opportunity for it; and moreover, our Saviour Christ promised: "Where two or three be gathered together in my name, there will I be in the midst of them."

When king David was idle and alone, and went not out to the wars, then he fell into adultery and murder. I myself have found that I never fell into more sin than when I was alone. God has created mankind for fellowship, and not for solitariness, which is clearly proved by this strong argument: God, in the creation of the world, created man and woman, to the end that the man in the woman should have a fellow.

· 436 ·

We find in no history any human creature oppressed with such sorrow as to sweat blood, therefore this history of Christ is wonderful; no man can understand or conceive what his bloody sweat is. And it is more wonderful, that the Lord of grace and of wrath, of life and of death, should be so weak, and made so sorrowful, as to be constrained to seek for solace and comfort of poor and miserable sinners, and to say: Ah, loving disciples! sleep not, wake yet a little, and talk one with another, that at least I may hear some people are about me. Here the Psalm was rightly applied, which says: "Thou hast made him a little lower than the angels," &c. Ah, that bloody sweat was pressed out of our blessed, sweet Saviour Christ Jesus, through the immeasurable heavy burden which lay on his innocent back; namely, the sins of the universal world, against which, doubtless, he prayed: "O Lord, rebuke me not in thine anger, neither chasten me in thy hot displeasure."

OF OFFENCES

· 437 ·

I may compare the state of a Christian to a goose, tied up over a wolf's pit to catch wolves. About the pit stand many ravening wolves, that would willingly devour the goose, but she is preserved alive, while they, leaping at her, fall into the pit, are taken and destroyed. Even so, we that are Christians are preserved by the sweet loving angels, so that the devils, those ravening wolves, the tyrants and persecutors, cannot destroy us.

· 438 ·

We little know how good and necessary it is for us to have adversaries, and for heretics to hold up their heads against us. For if Cerinthus had not been, then St. John the Evangelist had not written his gospel; but when Cerinthus opposed the godhead in our Lord Christ, John was constrained to write and say: In the beginning was the Word; making the distinction of the three persons so clear, that nothing could be clearer. So when I began to write against indulgences and against the pope, Dr. Eck set upon me, and aroused me out of my drowsiness. I wish from my heart this man might be turned the right way, and be converted; for that I would give one of my fingers; but if he will remain where he is, I wish he were made pope, for he has well deserved it, for hitherto he has had upon him the whole burthen of Popedom, in disputing and writing against me. Besides him, they have none that dare fall upon me; he raised my first cogitations against the pope, and brought me so far, or otherwise I never should have gone on.

· 439 ·

A liar is far worse, and does greater mischief, than a murderer on the highway; for a liar and false teacher deceives people, seduces souls, and destroys them under the color of God's Word; such a liar and murderer was Judas, like his father the devil. It was a marvel how Judas should sit at the table with Christ, and not blush for shame, when Christ said: "One of you shall betray me," &c. The other disciples had not the least thought that Judas would betray Christ; each was rather afraid of himself, thinking Christ meant him; for Christ trusted Judas with the purse, and the whole management of the house-keeping, whence he was held in great repute by the apostles.

· 440 ·

A scorpion thinks when his head lies hid under a leaf, that he cannot be seen; even so the hypocrites and false saints think, when they have hoisted up

one or two good works, that all their sins therewith
are covered and hid.

· 441 ·

False Christians that boast of the gospel, and yet
bring no good fruits, are like the clouds without
rain, wherewith the whole element is overshadowed,
gloomy and dark, and yet no rain falls to fructify
the ground: even so, many Christians affect great
sanctity and holiness, but they have neither faith
nor love towards God, nor love towards their neighbour.

· 442 ·

Job says: "The life of a human creature is a war-
fare upon earth." A human creature, especially a
Christian, must be a soldier, ever striving and fight-
ing with the enemy. And St. Paul describes the
armour of a Christian, Ephes. vi., thus:—

First—The girdle of truth; that is, the confession of the pure doctrine cf the gospel, an upright,
not a hypocritical or feigned faith.

Secondly—The breast-plate of righteousness, by
which is not meant the righteousness of a good
conscience, although this be also needful: for it is
written, "Enter not into judgment with thy servant,"

&c.; and St. Paul: "I know nothing of myself, yet I am not thereby justified," but the righteousness of faith, and of the remission of sins, which Paul means in that place, touching which Moses spake, Gen. xv.: "Abraham believed God, and that was imputed unto him for righteousness."

Thirdly—The shoes wherewith the feet are shod; viz. the works of the vocation, whereby we ought to remain, and not to go further, or to break out beyond the appointed mark.

Fourthly—The shield of faith; similar to this is the fable of Perseus with the head of Gorgon, upon which whoso looked died immediately; as Perseus held and threw Gorgon's head before his enemies, and thereby got the victory, even so a Christian must likewise hold and cast the Son of God, as Gorgon's head, before all the evil instigations and crafts of the devil, and then most certainly he shall prevail and get the victory.

Fifthly—The helmet of salvation; that is, the hope of everlasting life. The weapon wherewith a Christian fights the enemy is: "The sword of the spirit," 1 Thess. v., that is, God's word and prayer; for as the lion is frightened at nothing more than at the crowing of a cock, so the devil can be overcome and vanquished with nothing else than with

God's word and prayer; of this Christ himself has given us an example.

· 443 ·

Our life is like the sailing of a ship; as the mariners in the ship have before them a haven towards which they direct their course, and where they will be secure from all danger, even so the promise of everlasting life is made unto us, that we therein, as in a safe haven, may rest calm and secure. But seeing our ship is weak, and the winds and waves beat upon us, as though they would overwhelm us, therefore we have need of a good and experienced pilot, who with his counsel and advice may rule and govern the vessel, that it run not on a rock, or utterly sink and go down. Such a pilot is our blessed Saviour Christ Jesus.

· 444 ·

Ingratitude is a very irksome thing, which no human creature can tolerate; yet our Lord God can endure it. If I had had to do with the Jews, patience would have failed me; I had never been able so long to endure their stubbornness. The prophets were always poor, contemned people; plagued and persecuted not only by outward and open, but also by inward and secret enemies, for the most part of their own people. That which the pope does against us is nothing to compare with that which Jeckel and others do, to our sorrow of heart.

· 445 ·

We ought diligently to be aware of sophistry, which not only consists in doubtful and uncertain words, that may be construed and turned as one pleases, but also, in each profession, in all high arts, as in religion, covers and cloaks itself with the fair name of Holy Scripture, alleging to be God's word, and spoken from heaven. Those are unworthy of praise who can pervert everything, screwing, contemning, and rejecting the meanings and opinions of others, and, like the philosopher Carneades, disputing *in utraque parte,* and yet conclude nothing certain. These are knavish tricks and sophistical inventions. But a fine understanding, honestly disposed, that seeks after truth, and loves that which is plain and upright, is worthy of all honour and praise.

· 446 ·

Offences by Christians are far more abominable than those by the heathen. The prophet Jeremiah

says: "The punishment of the iniquity of the daughter of my people, is greater than the punishment
of the sin of Sodom," &c. And Ezekiel: "Thou hast
justified Sodom with thine abominations." And
Christ: "It will be more tolerable for Sodom at the
day of judgment, than with thee." But so it must
be: "He came unto his own, and his own received
him not." Truly this makes the godly altogether
faint and out of heart, so that they rather desire
death, for, with sorrow of heart, we find that many
of our people offend others. We ought diligently
to pray to God against offences, to the end his
name may be hallowed. St. Paul says: "Also of our
ownselves shall men arise, speaking perverse things,
to draw away disciples after them." Therefore the
church has no external esteem or succession; it
inherits not.

· 447 ·

True, much offence proceeds out of my doctrine;
but I comfort myself, as St. Paul did Titus: whereas
this doctrine is revealed for the sake of the faith
of God's chosen, for whose sake we also preach,
we mean it earnestly. For the sake of others I would
not drop one word. I have cracked many hollow
nuts, and yet I thought they had been good, but

they fouled my mouth, and filled it with dust; Carlstad and Erasmus are mere hollow nuts, and foul the mouth.

· 448 ·

It has been asked: Is an offence, committed in a moment of intoxication, therefore excusable? Most assuredly not; on the contrary, drunkenness aggravates the fault. Hidden sins unveil themselves when a man's self-possession goes from him; that which the sober man keeps in his breast, the drunken man lets out at the lips. Astute people, when they want to ascertain a man's true character, make him drunk. This same drunkenness is a grievous vice among us Germans, and should be heavily chastised by the temporal magistrate, since the fear of God will not suffice to keep the brawling guzzlers in check.

OF A CHRISTIAN LIFE

· 449 ·

A CHRISTIAN's worshipping is not the external, hypocritical mask that our spiritual friars wear, when they chastise their bodies, torment and make themselves faint, with ostentatious fasting, watching, singing, wearing hair shirts, scourging themselves, &c. Such worshipping God desires not.

· 450 ·

'Tis a great blindness of people's hearts that they cannot accept of the treasure of grace presented unto them. Such people are we, that though we are baptised, have Christ, with all his precious gifts, faith, the sacraments, his Word, all which we confess to be holy, yet we can neither say nor think that we ourselves are holy; we deem it too much to say, we are holy; whereas the name Christian is far more glorious and greater than the name holy.

· 451 ·

We can call consecrated robes, dead men's bones, and such trumpery, holy, but not a Christian; the reason is, we gaze upon the outward mask, we look after the seeming saint, who leads an austere life. Hence that vain opinion in Popedom, that they call the dead, saints; an error strengthened by Zuinglius. Human wisdom gapes at holy-workers, thinking whoso does good works, is just and righteous before God.

· 452 ·

There's no better death than St. Stephen's, who said: "Lord receive my spirit." We should lay aside the register of our sins and deserts, and die in reliance only upon God's mere grace and mercy.

· 453 ·

We ought to retain the feast of John the Baptist, with whom the New Testament began, for it is written: "All the prophets and the law prophesied until John," &c. We should observe it, too, for the sake of the fair song, which in Popedom we read, but understood not, of Zachariah, which, indeed, is a most excellent song, as is shown in St. Luke's preface, where he says: "And Zachariah was full of the Holy Ghost," &c.

· 454 ·

A householder instructs his servants and family in this manner: Deal uprightly and honestly, be diligent in that which I command you, and ye may then eat, drink, and clothe yourselves as ye please. Even so, our Lord God regards not what we eat, drink, or how we clothe ourselves; all such matters, being ceremonies or middle things, he leaves freely to us, on the understanding, however, that we

ground nothing thereon as being necessary to salvation.

· 455 ·

'Twas a strange thing the world should have been
offended at him who raised the dead, made the blind
to see, and the deaf to hear, &c. They who deem
such a man a devil, what manner of God would
they have? But here it is. Christ would give to
the world the kingdom of heaven, but they will have
the kingdom of the earth, and here they part; for
the highest wisdom and sanctity of the hypocrites
sees nothing but temporal honour, carnal will, mundane life, good days, money and wealth, all which
must vanish and cease.

· 456 ·

The whole world takes offence at the plainness of
the second table of God's ten commandments, because human sense and reason partly understand
what is done contrary thereto. When God and his
Word is contemned, the world is silent and regards
it not; but when a monastery is taken, or flesh eaten
on a Friday, or a friar marries, O, then the world
cries out: Here are abominable offences!

· 457 ·

The obedience towards God is the obedience of faith and good works; that is, he who believes in God, and does what God has commanded, is obedient unto him; but the obedience towards the devil is superstition and evil works; that is, who trusts not in God, but is unbelieving, and does evil, is obedient unto the devil.

· 458 ·

In the Old Testament are two sorts of sacrifices: the first was called the early morning sacrifice; thereby is shown that we first should offer unto Christ, not oxen or cattle, but ourselves, acknowledging God's gifts, corporal and spiritual, temporal and eternal, and giving him thanks for them. Secondly, the evening sacrifice; whereby is signified that a Christian should offer a broken, humble, and a contrite heart, consider his necessities and dangers, both corporal and spiritual, and call upon God for help.

· 459 ·

God will, say some, that we should serve him freely and willingly, whereas he that serves God out of fear of punishment, of hell, or out of a hope

and love of recompense, serves and honours God
not uprightly or truly. This argument is of the
stoics, who reject the affections of human nature. It
is true we ought willingly to serve, love, and fear
God, as the chief good. But God can well endure
that we love him for his promise' sake, and pray
unto him for corporal and spiritual benefits; he
therefore has commanded us to pray. So God can
also endure that we fear him for the punishment's
sake, as the prophets remember. Indeed, it is somewhat, that a human creature can acknowledge God's
everlasting punishment and rewards. And if one
looks thereupon, as not being the chief end and
cause, then it hurts him not, especially if he has
regard to God himself, as the final cause, who gives
everything for nothing, out of mere grace, without
our deserts.

· 460 ·

The word, to worship, means to stoop and bow
down the body with external gestures; to serve in
the work. But to worship God in spirit is the service
and honour of the heart; it comprehends faith and
fear in God. The worshipping of God is twofold,
outward and inward—that is, to acknowledge God's
benefits, and to be thankful unto him.

· 461 ·

A certain prince of Germany, well known to me, went to Compostella in Spain, where they pretend St. James, brother of the Evangelist St. John, lies buried. This prince made his confession to a Franciscan, an honest man, who asked him if he were a German? The prince answered, yes. Then the friar said: "O, loving child, why seekest thou so far away that which thou hast much better in Germany? I have seen and read the writings of an Augustin friar, touching indulgences and the pardons of sin, wherein he powerfully proves that the true remission of sins consists in the merits and sufferings of our Lord and Saviour Jesus Christ. O loving son, remain thereby, and permit not thyself to be otherwise persuaded. I purpose shortly, God willing, to leave this unchristian life, to repair into Germany, and to join the Augustin friar."

· 462 ·

Since the gospel has been preached, which is not above twenty years, such great wonders have been done as were not in many hundred years before. No man ever thought such alterations should happen; that so many monasteries should be made empty, that the private mass should be abolished in Germany, despite heretics, sectaries, and tyrants. Rome has twice been ravaged, and many great princes, who persecuted the gospel, have been thrown down to the ground and destroyed.

OF DISCORD

· 463 ·

THE 10th of February, 1546, John, prince elector of Saxony, said: A controversy were easily settled, if the parties would exhibit some concord. Luther said: We would willingly have concord, but no man seeks after the medium of concord, which is charity. We seek riches, but no man seeks after the right means how to be rich, namely, through God's blessing. We all desire to be saved, but the world refuses the means how to be saved—the Mediator Christ.

In former times potentates and princes referred their controversies to faithful people, and did not so readily thrust them into the lawyer's hands. When people desire to be reconciled and to come to an agreement, one party must yield, and give way to the other. If God and mankind should be reconciled and agreed, God must give over his right and justice, and must lay aside his wrath; and we, mankind, must also lay down our own righteousness, for we also would needs be gods in Paradise; we thought ourselves wise as God, through the serpent's seduction; then Christ was fain to make an agreement between us; he interposed in the cause, and would be a mediator between God and man; this Mediator for his pains got the portion of a peace-maker, namely, the cross; he that parts two fighters, commonly gets the hardest knocks for himself. Even so Christ suffered and presented us with his passion and death; he died for our sakes, and for the sake of our justification he arose again. Thus the generation of mankind became reconciled with God.

· 464 ·

When two goats meet upon a narrow bridge over deep water, how do they behave? neither of them can turn back again, neither can pass the other, because the bridge is too narrow; if they should thrust

one another, they might both fall into the water and
be drowned; nature, then, has taught them, that if
the one lays himself down and permits the other to
go over him, both remain without hurt. Even so people should rather endure to be trod upon, than to fall
into debate and discord one with another.

· 465 ·

A Christian, for the sake of his own person,
neither curses nor revenges himself; but faith curses
and revenges itself. To understand this rightly, we
must distinguish God and man, the person and
cause. In what concerns God and his cause, we
must have no patience, nor bless; as for example,
when the ungodly persecute the gospel, this touches
God and his cause, and then we are not to bless
or to wish good success, but rather to curse the
persecutors and their proceedings. Such is called
faith's cursing, which, rather than it would suffer
God's Word to be suppressed and heresy maintained, would have all creatures go to wreck; for
through heresy we lose God himself, Numbers, xvi.
But individuals personally ought not to revenge
themselves, but to suffer all things, and according to Christ's doctrine and the nature of love, to
do good to their enemies.

OF SICKNESSES,
AND OF THE
CAUSES THEREOF

· 466 ·

WHEN young children cry lustily, they grow well and rapidly, for through crying, the members and veins are stretched out, which have no other exercise.

· 467 ·

A question was put to Luther: How these two sentences in Scripture might be reconciled together; first, concerning the sick of the palsy, where Christ says: "Son, be of good cheer, thy sins be forgiven thee." Where Christ intimates that sin was the cause of the palsy, and of every sickness. Second, touching him that was born blind, where John says: "That neither he nor his parents had sinned." Luther answered: In these words Christ testifies that the blind had not sinned, and sin is not the cause of blindness, for only active sins, which one commits personally, are the cause of sicknesses and plagues, not original sin; therefore the sins which the sick of the palsy himself committed were the cause of his palsy, whereas original sin was not the cause of the blindness of him that was born blind, or all people must be born blind, or be sick of the palsy.

· 468 ·

Experience has proved the toad to be endowed with valuable qualities. If you run a stick through three toads, and, after having dried them in the sun, apply them to any pestilent tumour, they draw out all the poison, and the malady will disappear.

· 469 ·

The cramp is the lightest sickness, and I believe the falling sickness a piece of the cramp, the one in the head, the other in the feet and legs; when the person feeling either moves quickly, or runs, it vanishes.

· 470 ·

Sleep is a most useful and most salutary operation of nature. Scarcely any minor annoyance angers me more than the being suddenly awakened out of a pleasant slumber. I understand, that in Italy they torture poor people by depriving them of sleep. 'Tis a torture that cannot long be endured.

· 471 ·

The physicians in sickness consider only of what natural causes the malady proceeds, and this they cure, or not, with their physic. But they see not that often the devil casts a sickness upon one without any natural causes. A higher physic must be required to resist the devil's diseases; namely, faith and prayer, which physic may be fetched out of God's Word. The 31st Psalm is good thereunto, where David says: "Into thine hand I commit my spirit." This passage I learned, in my sickness, to correct; in the first translation, I applied it only to the hour of death: but it should be said: My health, my happiness, my life, misfortune, sickness, death, &c., stand all in thy hands. Experience testifies this: for when we think, now we will be joyful and merry, easy and healthy, God soon sends what makes us quite the contrary.

When I was ill at Schmalcalden, the physicians made me take as much medicine as though I had been a great bull. Alack for him that depends upon

the aid of physic. I do not deny that medicine is
a gift of God, nor do I refuse to acknowledge science in the skill of many physicians; but, take the
best of them, how far are they from perfection? A
sound regimen produces excellent effects. When I
feel indisposed, by observing a strict diet and going
to bed early, I generally manage to get round again,
that is, if I can keep my mind tolerably at rest.
I have no objection to the doctors acting upon certain theories, but, at the same time, they must not
expect us to be the slaves of their fancies. We find
Avicenna and Galen, living in other times and in
other countries, prescribing wholly different remedies for the same disorders. I won't pin my faith
to any of them, ancient or modern. On the other
hand, nothing can well be more deplorable than
the proceeding of those fellows, ignorant as they
are complaisant, who let their patients follow ex-
actly their own fancies; 'tis these wretches who
more especially people the graveyards. Able, cau-
tious, and experienced physicians, are gifts of God.
They are the ministers of nature, to whom human
life is confided; but a moment's negligence may
ruin everything. No physician should take a single
step, but in humility and the fear of God; they who
are without the fear of God are mere homicides.

I expect that exercise and change of air do more good than all their purgings and bleedings, but when we do employ medical remedies, we should be careful to do so under the advice of a judicious physician. See what happened to Peter Lupinus, who died from taking internally a mixture designed for external application. I remember hearing of a great law-suit, arising out of a dose of appium being given instead of a dose of opium.

· 472 ·

'Tis a curious thing that certain remedies, which, applied by princes and great lords, are efficacious and curative, are wholly powerless when administered by a physician. I have heard that the electors of Saxony, John and Frederic, have a water, which cures diseases of the eye, when they themselves apply it, whether the disorder arise from heat or from cold; but 'tis quite useless when administered by a physician. So in spiritual matters, a preacher has more unction, and produces more effect upon the conscience than can a layman.

OF DEATH

· 473 ·

To die for the sake of Christ's word, is esteemed precious and glorious before God. We are mortal, and must die for the sake of our sins, but when we die for the sake of Christ and his word, and freely confess them, we die an honourable death; we are thereby made altogether holy relics, and have sold our hides dear enough. But when we Christians pray for peace and long life, 'tis not for our sake, to whom death is merely gain, but for the sake of the church, and of posterity.

The fear of death is merely death itself; he who abolishes that fear from the heart, neither tastes nor feels death. A human creature lying asleep is very like one that is dead; whence the ancients said, sleep is the brother of death. In like manner, life and death are pictured to us in the day and night, and in the change and alteration of the seasons.

The dream I had lately, will be made true; 'twas that I was dead, and stood by my grave, covered with rags. Thus am I long since condemned to die, and yet I live.

· 474 ·

"Whoso keepeth my saying, shall never see death." Luther expounded this passage of St. John thus: We must die and suffer death, but whoso holds on God's Word, shall not feel death, but depart as in a sleep, and concerning him it shall not be said: "I die, but I am forced to sleep." On the other hand, whoso finds not himself furnished with God's Word, must die in anguish; therefore, when thou comest to die, make no dispute at all, but from thy heart say: I believe in Jesus Christ the Son of God; I ask no more.

· 475 ·

One's thirty-eighth year is an evil and dangerous year, bringing many heavy and great sicknesses: naturally, by reason, perhaps, of the comets and conjunctions of Saturn and of Mars, but spiritually, by reason of the innumerable sins of the people.

· 476 ·

Pliny, the heathen writer, says, book xx. cap. 1: The best physic for a human creature is, soon to die; Julius Cæsar contemned death, and was careless of danger; he said: 'Tis better to die once than continually to be afraid of dying; this was well enough for a heathen, yet we ought not to tempt God, but to use the means which he gives, and then commit ourselves to his mercy.

It were a light and easy matter for a Christian to overcome death, if he knew it was not God's wrath; that quality makes death bitter to us. But a heathen dies securely; he neither sees nor feels that it is God's wrath, but thinks it is merely the end of nature. The epicurean says: 'Tis but to endure one evil hour.

· 477 ·

When I hear that a good and godly man is dead, I am affrighted, and fear that God hates the world, and is taking away the upright and good, to the end he may fall upon and punish the wicked. Though I die, it makes no great matter; for I am in the pope's curse and excommunication; I am his devil, therefore he hates and persecutes me. At Coburg, I went about, and sought me out a place for my grave; I thought to have been laid in the chancel under the table, but now I am of another mind. I know I have not long to live, for my head

is like a knife, from which the steel is wholly
whetted away, and which is become mere iron; the
iron will cut no more, even so it is with my head.
Now, loving Lord God, I hope my time is not far
hence; God help me, and give me a happy hour;
I desire to live no longer.

· 478 ·

We read of St. Vincent, that, about to die, and
seeing death at his feet, he said: Death! what wilt
thou? Thinkest thou to gain anything of a Chris-
tion? Knowest thou not that I am a Christian?
Even so should we learn to contemn, scorn, and
deride death. Likewise, it is written in the history
of St. Martin, that being near his death, he saw
the devil standing at his bed's feet, and boldly said:
Why standest thou there, thou horrible beast? thou
hast nothing to do with me. These were right words
of faith. Such and the like ought we to cull out of
the legends of the saints, wholly omitting the fool-
eries that the papists have stuffed therein.

· 479 ·

Luther, at Wittenberg, seeing a very melancholy
man, said to him: Ah! human creature, what dost
thou? Hast thou nothing else in hand but to think

of thy sins, on death, and damnation? Turn thine
eyes quickly away, and look hither to this man
Christ, of whom it is written: "He was conceived
by the Holy Ghost, born of the Virgin Mary, suffered, died, buried, descended into hell, the third
day arose again from the dead, and ascended up
into heaven," &c. Dost think all this was done to
no end? Comfort thyself against death and sin;
be not afraid, nor faint, for thou hast no cause;
Christ suffered death for thee, and prevailed for thy
comfort and defence, and for that cause he sits at
the right hand of God, his heavenly Father, to deliver thee.

· 480 ·

So many members as we have, so many deaths
have we. Death peeps out at every limb. The devil,
a causer and lord of death, is our adversary, and
hunts after our life; he has sworn our death, and
we have deserved it; but the devil will not gain
much by strangling the godly; he will crack a hollow nut. Let us die, that so the devil may be at
rest. I have deserved death twofold; first, in that
I have sinned against God, for which I am heartily
sorry; secondly, I have deserved death at the devil's
hands, whose kingdom of lying and murdering,

through God's assistance, grace, and mercy, I have destroyed; therefore he justly wishes my death.

· 481 ·

"There shall arise false prophets, insomuch that, if it were possible, they shall deceive the very elect." This sentence was fulfilled, in the fathers; as in Jerome, Augustin, Gregory, Bernard, and others; they were seduced into errors, but remained not therein. St. Bernard wrote many evil and ungodly things, especially concerning the Virgin Mary; but when he was near his death, he said: "I have lived wickedly. Thou, loving Lord Jesus Christ, hast a twofold right to the kingdom of heaven; first, it is thine inheritance, for thou art the only begotten Son of the Father; this affords me no comfort or hope of heaven. But, secondly, thou hast purchased the same with thy suffering and death; thou hast stilled the Father's wrath, hast unlocked heaven, and presented the same unto me as thy purchased good; of this have I joy and comfort." Therefore he died well and happy. Likewise when St. Augustin was to die, he prayed the seven penitential psalms. When these fathers were in health, they thought not on this doctrine; but when they were upon their death-beds, they found in their hearts what they were to trust to; they felt it high time to abandon human fopperies, and to betake themselves only to Christ, and to rely upon his rich and precious merits.

· 482 ·

Almighty, everlasting God, merciful heavenly Father, Father of our loving Lord Jesus Christ, I know assuredly, that everything which thou hast said, thou wilt and canst perform, for thou canst not lie; thy Word is upright and true. In the beginning, thou didst promise unto me thy loving and only begotten Son Jesus Christ; the same is come, and has delivered me from the devil, from death, hell, and sin. Out of his gracious will he has presented unto me the sacraments, which I have used in faith, and have depended on thy word; wherefore I make no doubt at all, but that I am well secured, and settled in peace; therefore if this be my hour, and thy divine will, so am I willing to depart hence with joy.

· 483 ·

The school of faith is said to go about with death. Death is swallowed up in victory. If death, then sin. If death, then all diseases. If death, then all misery. If death, then all the power of the devil. If death, then all the fury of the world.

But these things do not appear, but rather the contrary; therefore there is need of faith; for an open manifestation of things follows faith in due time, when the things, now invisible, will be seen.

· 484 ·

When Adam lived, that is, when he sinned, death devoured life; when Christ died, that is, was justified, then life, which is Christ, swallowed up and devoured death; therefore God be praised, that Christ died, and has got the victory.

OF THE
RESURRECTION

· 485 ·

On Easter Sunday, 1544, Luther made an excellent sermon on the resurrection from the dead, out of the epistle appointed for that day, handling this sentence: "Thou fool, that which thou sowest is not quickened except it die." When Abraham intended to sacrifice his son, he believed that God out of the ashes would raise him again, and make him a father of children. The faith of Adam and of Eve preserved them, because they trusted and believed in the promised seed. For to him that believes everything is possible. The conception and birth of every human creature, proceeding out of a drop of blood, is no less a miracle and wonder-work of God, than that Adam was made out of a clod of earth, and Eve out of a fleshy rib. The world is full of such works of wonder, but we are blind, and cannot see them. The whole world is not able to create one member, no, not so much as a small leaf. The manner of the resurrection consists in these words: "Arise, come, stand up, appear, rejoice ye which dwell in the dust of the earth." I shall arise again, and shall speak with you; this finger wherewith I point must come to me again; everything must come again; for it is written: "God will create a new heaven and a new earth, wherein righteousness shall dwell." It will be no arid waste, but a beautiful new earth, where all the just will dwell together. There will be no carnivorous beasts, or venomous creatures, for all such, like ourselves, will be relieved from the curse of sin, and will be to us as friendly as they were to Adam in Paradise. There will be little dogs, with golden hair, shining like precious stones. The foliage of the trees, and the verdure of the grass, will have the brilliancy of emeralds; and we ourselves, delivered from our mundane subjection to gross appetites and necessities, shall have the same form as here, but infinitely more perfect. Our eyes will be radiant as the purest silver, and we shall be exempt from all sickness and tribulation. We shall behold the glorious Creator face to face; and then, what ineffable satisfaction will it be to find our relations and friends among the just! If we were all one here, we should have peace among ourselves, but God orders it otherwise, to the end we may yearn and sigh after the future paternal home, and become weary of this troublesome life. Now, if there be joy in the chosen, so must the highest sorrow and despair be in the damned.

· 486 ·

The 7th of August, 1538, Luther discoursed concerning the life to come, and said: In my late sickness I lay very weak, and committed myself to God,

when many things fell into my mind, concerning
the everlasting life, what it is, what joys we there
shall have, and I was convinced that everything
shall be revealed, which through Christ is presented
unto us, and is already ours, seeing we believe it.
Here on earth we cannot know what the creation of
the new world shall be, for we are not able to
comprehend or understand the creation of this temporal world, or of its creatures, which are visible
and corporal. The joys that are everlasting are
beyond the comprehension of any human creature.
As Isaiah says: *"Ye shall be everlastingly joyful
in glorious joy."* But how comes it that we cannot
believe God's Word, seeing that all things are accomplished which the Scripture speaks touching the
resurrection of the dead? This proves original sin
as the cause of it. The ungodly and damned at the
last day shall be under the ground, but in some
measure shall behold the great joys and glory of
the chosen and saved, and thereby shall be so much
the more pained and tormented.

Has our Lord God created this evanescent and
temporal kingdom, the sky, and earth, and all that
is therein, so fair; how much more fair and glorious
will he, then, make yonder celestial everlasting
kingdom.

· 487 ·

When I lay sucking at my mother's breasts, I had
no notion how I should afterwards eat, drink, or
live. Even so we on earth have no idea what the life
to come will be.

· 488 ·

I hold the gnashing of teeth of the damned to be
an external pain following upon an evil conscience,
that is, despair, when men see themselves abandoned by God.

· 489 ·

I wish from my heart Zuinglius could be saved,
but I fear the contrary; for Christ has said, that
those who deny him shall be damned. God's judgment is sure and certain, and we may safely pronounce it against all the ungodly, unless God reserve
unto himself a peculiar privilege and dispensation.
Even so, David from his heart wished that his son
Absalom might be saved, when he said: "Absalom
my son, Absalom my son," yet he certainly believed
that he was damned, and bewailed him, not only
in that he died corporally, but was also lost everlastingly; for he knew that he died in rebellion, in

incest, and that he had hunted his father out of the kingdom.

· 490 ·

The Fathers made four sorts of hell. 1. The forefront, wherein, they say, the patriarchs were until Christ descended into hell. 2. The feeling of pain, yet only temporal, as purgatory. 3. Where unbaptized children are, but feel no pain. 4. Where the damned are, which feel everlasting pain. This is the right hell; the other three are only human imaginings. In Popedom they sang an evil song: "Our sighs called upon thee, our pitiful lamentations sought thee," &c. This was not Christianlike, for the gospel says: "They are in Abraham's bosom." Isaiah: "They go into their chambers;" and Ecclesiasticus: "The righteous is in the Lord's hand, let him die how he will, yea, although he be overtaken by death." What hell is, we know not; only this we know, that there is such a sure and certain place, as is written of the rich glutton, when Abraham said unto him: "There is a great space between you and us."

· 491 ·

Ah! loving God, defer not thy coming. I await

impatiently the day when the spring shall return, when day and night shall be of equal length, and when Aurora shall be clear and bright. One day will come a thick black cloud, out of which will issue three flashes of lightning, and a clap of thunder will be heard, and, in a moment, heaven and earth will be covered with confusion. The Lord be praised, who has taught us to sigh and yearn after that day. In Popedom they are all afraid thereof, as is testified by their hymn, *Dies iræ dies illa.* I hope that day is not far off. Christ says: "At that time, ye shall scarcely find faith on the earth." If we make an account, we shall find, that we have the gospel now only in a corner. Asia and Africa have it not, the gospel is not preached in Europe, in Greece, Italy, Hungary, Spain, France, England, or in Poland. And this little corner where it is, Saxony, will not hinder the coming of the last day of judgment. The predictions of the apocalypse are accomplished already, as far as the white horse. The world cannot stand long, perhaps a hundred years at the outside.

When the Turk begins to decline, then the last day will be at hand, for then the testimony of the Scripture must be verified. The loving Lord will come, as the Scripture says: "For thus saith the

Lord of Hosts, yet a little while and I will shake the heavens and the earth, and the sea and the dry land: and I will shake all nations, and the desire of all nations shall come." At the last there will be great alteration and commotion; and already there are great commotions among men. Never had the men of law so much occupation as now. There are vehement dissensions in our families, and discord in the church.

· 492 ·

About the time of Easter in April, when they least of all feared rain, Pharaoh was swallowed up in the Red Sea, and the nation of Israel delivered from Egypt. 'Twas at about the same time the world was created; at the same time the year is changed, and at the same time Christ arose again to renew the world. Perchance the last day will come about the same time. I am of opinion it will be about Easter, when the year is finest and fairest, and early in the morning, at sunrise, as at the destruction of Sodom and Gomorrah. The elements will be gloomy with earthquakes and thunderings about an hour or a little longer, and the secure people will say: "Pish, thou fool, hast thou never heard it thunder?"

· 493 ·

The science of alchemy I like very well, and, indeed, 'tis the philosophy of the ancients. I like it not only for the profits it brings in melting metals, in decocting, preparing, extracting, and distilling herbs, roots; I like it also for the sake of the allegory and secret signification, which is exceedingly fine, touching the resurrection of the dead at the last day. For, as in a furnace the fire extracts and separates from a substance the other portions, and carries upward the spirit, the life, the sap, the strength, while the unclean matter, the dregs, remain at the bottom, like a dead and worthless carcass; even so God, at the day of judgment, will separate all things through fire, the righteous from the ungodly. The Christians and righteous shall ascend upwards into heaven, and there live everlastingly, but the wicked and the ungodly, as the dross and filth, shall remain in hell, and there be damned.

OF UNIVERSITIES,
ARTS, ETC.

· 494 ·

A LAWYER is wise according to human wisdom, a divine according to God's wisdom.

· 495 ·

Ah! how bitter an enemy is the devil to our church and school here at Wittenberg, which in particular he opposes more than the rest, so that tyranny and heresy increase and get the upper hand by force, in that all the members of the church are against one another; yea, also we, which are a piece of the heart, vex and plague one another among ourselves. I am verily persuaded that many wicked wretches and spies are here, who watch over us with an evil eye, and are glad when discord and offences arise among us; therefore we ought diligently to watch and pray; it is high time—pray, pray. This school is a foundation and ground of pure religion, therefore she ought justly to be preserved and maintained with lectures and with stipends against the raging and swelling of Satan.

· 496 ·

Whoso after my death shall contemn the authority of this school here at Wittenberg, if it remain as it is now, church and school, is a heretic and a perverted creature; for in this school God first revealed and purified his word. This school and city, both in doctrine and manner of life, may justly be compared with all others; yet we are not altogether complete, but still faulty in our kind of living. The highest and chiefest divines in the whole empire hold and join with us—as Amsdorf, Brentius, and Rhegius—all desiring our friendship, and saluting us with loving and learned letters. A few years past, nothing was of any value but the pope, till the church mourned, cried, and sighed, and awakened our Lord God in heaven; as in the Psalm he says: "For the trouble of the needy and the groans of the poor, I will now arise."

· 497 ·

Our nobility exhaust people with usury, insomuch that many poor people starve for want of food; the

cry goes, I would willingly take a wife, if I knew
how to maintain her, so that a forced celibacy will
hence ensue. This is not good; such wicked courses
will cause the poor to cry and sigh, will rouse up
God and the heavenly host. Wherefore I say: Germany, take heed. I often make an account, and as I
come nearer and nearer to forty years, I think with
myself: now comes an alteration, for St. Paul
preached not above forty years, nor St. Augustin;
always, after forty years pure preaching of God's
Word, it has ceased, and great calamities have en-
sued thereupon.

· 498 ·

Dialectica speaks simply, straightforward, and
plainly, as when I say: Give me something to drink.
But *Rhetorica* adorns the matter, saying: Give me
of the acceptable juice in the cellar, which finely
froths and makes people merry. *Dialectica* declares
a thing distinctly and significantly, in brief words.
Rhetorica counsels and advises, persuades and dis-
suades; she has her place and fountain-head, whence
a thing is taken; as, this is good, honest, profitable, easy, necessary, &c. These two arts St. Paul
briefly taught, where he says: "That he may be able

by sound doctrine, both to exhort and to convince the gainsayers." (Tit. 1.) Therefore, when I would teach a farmer concerning the tilling of his land, I define briefly and plainly, his kind of life; his housekeeping, fruits, profits, and all that belongs to the being of his life, *Dialecticè*; but, if I would admonish him, according to *Rhetorica*, then I counsel and advise him, and praise his kind of life, in this manner, as: that it is the most quiet, the richest, securest, and most delightful kind of life, &c. Again, if I intend to chide or to find fault, then I must point out and blame his misconduct, evil impediments, failings, gross ignorance, and such like defects which are in the state of farmers. Philip Melancthon has illustrated and declared good arts: he teaches them in such sort, that the arts teach not him, but he the arts; I bring my arts into books, I take them not out of books. *Dialectica* is a profitable and necessary art, which justly ought to be studied and learned; it shows how we ought to speak orderly and uprightly, what we should acknowledge and judge to be right or wrong; 'tis not only necessary in schools, but also in consistories, in courts of justice, and in churches; in churches most especially.

· 499 ·

I always loved music; whoso has skill in this art, is of a good temperament, fitted for all things. We must teach music in schools; a schoolmaster ought to have skill in music, or I would not regard him; neither should we ordain young men as preachers, unless they have been well exercised in music.

· 500 ·

Singing has nothing to do with the affairs of this world, it is not for the law; singers are merry and free from sorrow and cares.

· 501 ·

Music is one of the best arts; the notes give life to the text; it expels melancholy, as we see in king Saul. Kings and princes ought to maintain music, for great potentates and rulers should protect good and liberal arts and laws; though private people have desire thereunto and love it, yet their ability is not adequate. We read in the Bible, that the good and godly kings maintained and paid singers. Music is the best solace for a sad and sorrowful mind; by it the heart is refreshed and settled again in peace.

OF LEARNED MEN

· 502 ·

LUTHER advised all who proposed to study, in what art soever, to read some sure and certain books over and over again; for to read many sorts of books produces rather confusion than any distinct result; just as those that dwell everywhere, and remain in no place, dwell nowhere, and have no home. As we use not daily the community of all our friends, but of a select few, even so we ought to accustom ourselves to the best books, and to make them familiar unto us, so as to have them, as we say, at our fingers' end. A fine talented student fell into a frenzy; the cause of his disease was, that he laid himself out too much upon books, and was in love with a girl. Luther dealt very mildly and friendly with him, expecting amendment, and said: Love is the cause of his sickness; study brought upon him but little of his disorder. In the beginning of the gospel it went so with myself.

· 503 ·

Who could be so mad, in these evil times, as to write history and the truth? The brains of the Greeks were subtle and crafty; the Italians are ambitious and proud; the Germans rude and boisterous. Livy described the acts of the Romans, not of the Carthaginians. Blandus and Platina only flatter the popes.

· 504 ·

Anno 1536 Luther wrote upon his tablets the following words: *Res et verba Philippus; verba sine re Erasmus; res sine verbis Lutherus; nec res, nec verba Carolostadius;* that is, what Philip Melancthon writes has hands and feet; the matter is good, and the words are good; Erasmus Roterodamus writes many words, but to no purpose; Luther has good matter, but the words are wanting; Carlstad has neither good words nor good matter. Philip Melancthon coming in at the moment, read these criticisms, and turning with a smile to Dr. Basil, said: Touching Erasmus and Carlstad, 'twas well said, but too much praise is accorded to me, while good words ought to be reckoned among the other merits of Luther, for he speaks exceeding well, and has substantial matter.

· 505 ·

Luther, reproving Dr. Mayer, for that he was faint-hearted and depressed, by reason of his simple kind of preaching, in comparison with other divines, as he conceived, admonished him, and said: Loving brother, when you preach, regard not the doctors and learned men, but regard the common people, to teach and instruct them clearly. In the pulpit, we must feed the common people with milk, for each day a new church is growing up, which stands in need of plain and simple instruction. Keep to the catechism, the milk. High and subtle discourse, the strong wine, we will keep for the strong minded.

· 506 ·

No theologian of our time handles and expounds the Holy Scripture so well as Brentius, so much so that I greatly admire his energy, and despair of equalling him. I verily believe none among us can compare with him in the exposition of St. John's gospel; though, now and then, he dwells somewhat too much upon his own opinions, yet he keeps to the true and just meaning, and does not set himself up against the plain simplicity of God's Word.

· 507 ·

The discourse turning upon the great differences amongst the learned, Luther said: God has very finely distributed his gifts, so that the learned serve the unlearned, and the unlearned humble themselves before the learned, in what is needful for them. If all people were equal, the world could not go on; nobody would serve another, and there would be no peace. The peacock complained because he had not the nightingale's voice. God, with apparent inequality, has instituted the greatest equality; one man, who has greater gifts than another, is proud and haughty, and seeks to rule and domineer over others, and contemns them. God finely illustrates human society in the members of the body, and shows that one member must assist the other, and that none can be without the other.

· 508 ·

Aristotle is altogether an epicurean; he holds that God heeds not human creatures, nor regards how we live, permitting us to do at our pleasure. According to him, God rules the world as a sleepy maid rocks a child. Cicero got much further. He collected together what he found good in the books of all the Greek writers. 'Tis a good argument, and has often moved me much, where he proves there is a God, in that living creatures, beasts, and mankind engender their own likeness. A cow always produces a cow; a horse, a horse, &c. Therefore it follows that some being exists which rules everything. In God we may acknowledge the unchangeable and certain motion of the stars of heaven; the sun each day rises and sets in his place; as certain as time, we have winter and summer, but as this is done regularly, we neither admire nor regard it.